1 — Symbols and Concepts used in Linguist Can

2 — The 10 Phonics-based Spelling Books for all Ages by Camilia Sadik

3 — The 30 Unique Learning Features that Make Learning Inescapable

4   Who benefits from these phonics-based spelling books?

5   How to Teach from Each Book?

6   How to Explain This Learning Methodology to Students?

7   Comprehensive pre- and post-spelling tests

8

For Free Sample Lessons from each Book, visit SpellingRules.com

10 Phonics-based Spelling Books for All Ages

Students need to be familiar with these symbols and concepts used in the 10 phonics-based spelling books by Camilia Sadik:

Dots

Dots inside words indicate a division of words into syllables, as in "win·dow."

Italic Letters

Italic letters represent silent letters, like the italic silent "p" in "recei*p*t."

Meaning of Vowels

Vowels are **a**, **e**, **i**, **o**, **u**, sometimes "**y**" as in "sky," and sometimes "**w**" as in "f*e*w." Note that the "e" is silent in "f*e*w" and the only sound heard is the vowel "**u**" sound. Think of the "**w**" in "f*e*w" as if it were a "double **u**." Vowels are the letters that have sounds.

Long Vowels

Long vowels' symbols are ā, ē, ī, ō, and ū. A vowel is said to have a long sound when it sounds like its letter name. The ā, ē, ī, ō, and ū are as in main, meat, tie, boat, and venue.

Short Vowels

Short vowels' symbols are ă, ĕ, ĭ, ŏ, and ŭ. Each vowel has a distinctive short sound that is unique to that vowel. The ă, ĕ, ĭ, ŏ, and ŭ are as in mad, med, mid, mod, and mud.

Meaning of Consonants

Consonants are b, c, d, f, g, h, j, k, l, m, n, p, q, r, s, t, v, w, x, y, and z. The eight consonants c, g, h, q, s, x, w, and y are inconsistent and they produce **50** sounds, which are spelled in **60** spelling patterns. Consonants are the letters that do not have sounds unless they are paired with a vowel sound.

The Difference between Vowels and Consonants

1. Vowels have sounds, while consonants like the "b" are soundless unless they are said with a vowel; vowels are responsible for the sounds we make in our speech.

2. Vowels rule English and they cannot be avoided. Because they are the most inconsistent letters, vowels must be taken seriously. The five vowels alone produce 38 sounds, which are spelled in 96 ways. Learning all the inconsistencies in the vowels is the most important part of learning to read and spell. Consequently, the author dissected and isolated each vowel in a book.

3. Vowels help each other and there are several rules that govern the spelling of vowels in words. For instance and as in t**o**e, the silent "*e*" is there to help the "**o**" sound long.

4. Vowels are the strong letters and consonants are the weak letters. For instance, one consonant between two vowels, like the one "t" in "fat**e**," is too weak to keep the two vowels from helping each other. Therefore, we double the "t" in "fa**tt**er." We need two consonants between two vowels to prevent the vowels from helping each other. Now we know why there are so many double consonants.

5. Vowels are Inconsistent: Learning all the inconsistencies in the vowels, without logical explanations or spelling rules, is particularly difficult for students with a logical learning style. Lack of understanding how English vowels are structured can lead to poor spelling and poor reading skills among those who cannot memorize without logic.

Meaning of a Syllable

Examples of syllables: There are two syllables in "win·dow," "win" and "dow." There is only one syllable in the word "cak**e**." There are three syllables in "i·de·a." There are five syllables in "so·phis·ti·cat·ed." There are three syllables in "b**eau**·ti·ful."

Meaning of a syllable: A syllable can be a small word like the word "**me**" or a part of a word like the "me" in "**me**·di·a."

Only one vowel sound can be in a syllable: A syllable may contain one or more than one vowel, but it cannot have more than one vowel sound. It is not the number of vowels in a syllable that matters, as long as those vowels make one sound.

For instance, the syllable "b**eau**" in "b**eau**·ti·ful" contains three vowels, but only one vowel sound is heard, namely the sound of "u" is heard, and the vowels "*e*" and "*a*" in "b**eau**" are silent vowels–the "*e*" and "*a*"" do not count here because they are silent vowels and cannot break free to form a new syllable.

Likewise, there is only one vowel sound in "cak**e**" and the only vowel sound heard in "cak**e**" is the "a" sound because the "*e*" is silent. Because the "*e*" is silent in "cak**e**," the word "cak**e**" cannot be divided into "ca" and "k**e**" because "k**e**" would be soundless, therefore the silent "*e*" cannot count as a sounding vowel to form another syllable.

Meaning of a Schwa

A schwa is a name given to a weak sound of any vowel–it is this weak sound of a vowel that is often confused with a different vowel sound. For instance, the "a" sound in "sep·a·rate'" is weak; thus, it is often confused with an "e" sound. It is this weak sound of an "a" that is called a "schwa" sound. The stress in a word is on other syllables, but not on the syllable where the schwa is. The dictionary symbol for the schwa looks like this upside-down **e**: ə. Again, a schwa is the unstressed vowel sound in a word, which is vaguely heard. Examples of schwas are as in sep·a·rate', sou·ve·nir', cred'·i·ble, mem'·o·ry, and vir'·us.

Meaning of Phonics

Phonics is a group of English sounds produced by a single letter or by a combination of letters. Precisely, a phonic is a single sound produced by either a plain letter like the "f" in "fast" or by a combination of letters like the "ph" in "geography" or by a single letter that does not sound like its letter name like the "y" in "sky." Additional examples of phonics are as in auto, separate, culture, action, ocean, social, meat, Europe, lucky, ski, memory, and choir.

Meaning of Learning Phonics

The term "learning phonics" is not usually used to mean learning the ABC's. Typically, the use of the term "learning phonic" refers to learning the sounds produced by combinations of letters like the "sion" in "expression" and by letters that do not sound like their letter name like the "o" in "choir." Sadik's books are for learning nearly all of the combinations of letters and just about all of the letters that do not sound like their letter name in 32,000 words.

There are over 90 sounds we call phonics, which are spelled in over 180 ways we call spelling patterns. Learning the 26 plain letters and using them in words like "fast" is the easy part of learning to read and spell. More difficult is learning to use the letter combinations and the letters that do not sound like their letter name. Learning phonics means identifying which letter or combination of letters to choose when spelling every English sound in every English word.

When the spelling of phonics in English words is based strictly on memorization, logical learners whose learning style is a logical learning style, usually have various types of difficulties in spelling or in reading or in both.

However and after the discovery of over 100 spelling rules, logical learners have been learning the spelling of hundreds of words at a time. When dyslexic persons learned phonics logically, they proved they were not learning disabled and that their learning style was a logical style.

Phonics and Vowels

Each vowel has several sounds that are spelled in a number of ways. For instance, the vowel "e" has **seven** sounds that are spelled in **17** spelling patterns, as in these examples:

1. Short ĕ: red, bread

2. Long ē: meat, meet, Pete, chief, belief, monkey, lucky, he, ski, elite

3. Minor sounds of **e:** enough, eight, break, cake

4. Schwa sound of **e:** poet.

Teach Reading Phonics before Reading Comprehension

Choosing the correct spelling pattern in every English word is just as important as choosing the correct letter–and teaching only some spelling patterns, is like teaching some of the letters. It is unacceptable to teach only "some" of the 26 letters and then expect students to read and spell using all of the 26 letters. Likewise, it is unacceptable to teach only bits and pieces of phonics, and then expect students to read and spell. Teaching phonics is like teaching the rest of the alphabet. To ensure all types of learners read and spell, each spelling pattern of a sound must be learned beforehand similar to the way each letter is learned before reading words and sentences.

In addition to learning isolated spelling patterns, learning phonics means learning all of the spelling patterns of phonics in all of the words that contain that phonic. Reality is that less than 50% of any population can memorize without logic, and the rest are analyzers whose learning style is a logical learning style. Logical learners cannot memorize without logic, and they question why a single sound should be spelled one-way, and not the other. Logical learners expect to see "My cat is cute." to be, "Mi kat iz qut."

The Semivowels Theory by Camilia Sadik

Usually, vowels have sounds and consonants are soundless unless they are paired with a vowel sound. However and in spite of being consonants, the letters l, m, n, r, and s have some sounds of their own; thus, they can sometime act like vowels and have various effects on the vowels that precede them. For instances, the semivowels **l, m, n, r, and** s make the vowels that precede them long, as in fold, comb, mind, sort, and taste.

R-controlled words: As in "beggar," the semivowel "r" is particularly controlling of the vowels that precede it, and it is responsible for the vast majority of the schwa sounds. Also, semivowels can cause the preceding vowels to sound like another vowel. For instance, the "u" sound in "burn" is not a short vowel nor is it a schwa sound. More examples of r-controlled words are as in vulgar, liar, parole, virus, choir, tomorrow, purse, curb, word, ward, fur, fir, girl, part, etc.

Sight words explained: What was referred to as "sight words" is now explained by this *Semivowels Theory.* A semivowel follows and affects a preceding vowel in these so-called "sight words": mild, child, hold, old, sold, climb, comb, whom, mind, pint, ninth, change, union, virus, choir, Christ, most, etc. The *Semivowels Theory* is in Lesson 71 in *100 Spelling Rules.*

Book 1: *Read Instantly* **(200 Comprehensive Phonics Lessons for all Ages)**

Click to **LOOK INSIDE!**

Read Instantly by Camilia Sadik is a 152-page colored textbook and workbook. It is the first book in a series of ten. This specific book is for beginners who have not yet learned phonics or for those who missed learning phonics when they were growing up. Beginners may be any age and can be those who cannot yet read any words or those who can read but cannot spell the words that they read. *Read Instantly* is for all ages and all types of learners.

Comprehensive Phonics: Unlike most books that teach bits and pieces of phonics, *Read Instantly* is a comprehensive book of phonics. Its 200 phonics lessons cover over 180 spelling patterns of more than 90 sounds we call phonics in 1,400 basic but essential words. In it lies the foundation for learning the rules that govern the reading and spelling of phonics.

Placed in a Queue: Initially, 180 spelling patterns of the 90 sounds we call phonics are placed in a queue awaiting their turn to be introduced logically, one-at-a-time, and in a group of 20 to 50 words.

5

Comprehensive Vowels: Each vowel is dissected and isolated in a chapter in the second half of *Read Instantly*. Every sound and spelling pattern of a vowel is introduced step-by-step in a group of 30 to 50 words. The second half of *Read Instantly* is a mini version of the comprehensive book of vowels entitled *Learn to Spell 500 Words a Day*.

■ Why *Read Instantly*?

1. For Reading: *Read Instantly* is for anyone capable of learning the ABC's and cannot yet read for any reason. All learners capable of learning the English alphabet are guaranteed to learn to read from this book.

2. For Spelling: Children and adults with spelling difficulties need to start with this book to learn phonics and the basic rules that govern phonics, even if they can read and comprehend. *Read Instantly* is the foundation for reading phonics and for spelling basic words; it cannot be avoided. In addition to learning to read from *Read Instantly*, students learn to spell from it too. These books are cumulative and skipping *Read Instantly* is like forcing a baby to run before she or he can crawl or walk. If you stumble when reading aloud, you definitely need this book for spelling and to build a foundation for learning phonics.

3. For Logical Learners: Learners with spelling difficulties learn differently; their learning style is a logical learning style. They need logical explanations or spelling rules before they can memorize the spelling of words. Children or adults with spelling difficulties in English are logical learners and they need to start with *Read Instantly* to learn the basic rules that govern phonics, even if they can read and comprehend.

4. For All Types of Learners: *Read Instantly* works for K-3, older children, adult learners, dyslexic persons, brain-injured persons, and ESL students.

5. For Parents and Teachers of K-3: *Read Instantly* is the book for parents to teach reading before sending kids to school and for teachers to teach the foundation of phonics and phonics rules in K-3.

6. For Reversing Dyslexia: If anyone was forced into speed-reading before learning to spell words, there is no doubt that that person has dyslexia in spelling and in writing letters in reverse. Using *Read Instantly* is the first step toward reversing dyslexia or ending it among those who have it. You may read *What is dyslexia?* by Camilia Sadik. Dyslexic learners must slow down to write words slowly for a year or two. In time, they will acquire the ability to speed-read again naturally and without force.

7. For Preventing Dyslexia: In addition to reversing dyslexia, this is the book for teachers or parents to prevent dyslexia before the 3rd grade. Traditional reading programs that advocate speed-reading too soon, give our kids dyslexia before the 3rd grade. Read *How do you get dyslexia?* by Camilia Sadik.

8. For Brain-injured Persons: *Read Instantly* has been used to teach reading and spelling to countless brain-injured students, and they learned to read and spell instantly from it. Apparently, brain-injured persons become logical learners, *Read Instantly* was not intentionally written for them, but it has been working for them.

9. For ESL Students: English language learners have been reading phonics from this book even when they don't know the meaning of the words they are reading–they learn phonics similar to the way natives learn the ABC's, which have no meaning as letters standing alone. For example, they learn to read "tion" as in "action" even if they don't know the meaning of the word "action." After learning to read "action," they look up its meaning in their dictionaries.

■ **30 Unique Learning Features in *Read Instantly*:** The 30 unique learning features used in Camilia Sadik's books make learning to read and spell inescapable. All ages and all types of learners learn to read and spell. A few such features in *Read Instantly* are:

The Order of Lessons Introduced: The order of the lessons presented in *Read Instantly* is carefully planned and lessons build gradually. No words are thrown randomly at people to read or spell; instead, every phonic is initially placed in a queue awaiting its turn to be introduced logically, one-at-a-time, and in a group of 20 to 50 words.

The Informing before Introducing Approach: The principal of **I**nforming **b**efore **I**ntroducing a phonic is applied throughout *Read Instantly*. No student is asked to read or spell a phonic that has not been introduced beforehand. For instance, a word like "my" is introduced only after informing learners that the final "y" can sound like an "i" in small one-syllable words. Another example is that only after informing, are students asked to read words that contain silent letters. And, all the silent letters are italicized in this book as in: *k*not, *k*nob, *k*nit, lo*dg*e, dum*b*, bom*b*.

■ **Sample Lesson from *Read Instantly*:**
» **To teachers: I**nform **b**efore **I**ntroducing a new spelling patterns of phonics, as in:
• The initial "y" is a consonant at the beginning of words or syllables: you, ro·yal
• The final "y" in short words becomes a long ī: by, my, fly, why
• The final "y" in longer words becomes a long ē: happy, history
• The final "ey" becomes a long ē in approximately 40 English nouns: key, monkey, valley
• The final "ay" becomes a long ā: play, day, stay
• The special sound of ōy: boy, toy, joy, enjoy
• The stressed "y" at the end of a syllable is a long ī: by·pass
• The "y" inside a syllable can be a short ĭ: Lynn, gym, gymnasium

» **To students:** Read aloud to memorize and read slowly to see the way words are spelled:
• my, why, by, sly, shy
• funny, happy, happily, carry, hurry
• key, donkey, monkey, valley, alley
• day, play, way, tray, say
• boy, toy, employ, joy, enjoy

Phonics lessons in *Read Instantly* are short and less intimidating. For instance, the "ai" phonic is initially presented in 20 words, but at a later chapter, it is presented in 50 words. The same "ai" phonic is presented in 210 words in *Learn to Spell 500 Words a Day*.

■ Guaranteed Learning from *Read Instantly*:

Guaranteed Reading: Most adults and older children finish reading this entire 152-page book aloud in days or weeks. While reading this book, all will see huge results in the first hour or two. Anyone capable of learning the ABC's is guaranteed to learn to read and spell 20 words an hour from *Read Instantly*. Very young children in kindergarten may take a few months to finish reading *Read Instantly* because of their short attention span.

Read Instantly has been successfully used by parents, homeschooling parents, adult learners, and by teachers as a resource book to teach reading to K-3 kids. However, it functions as a self-help spelling book for those who can read but cannot spell the words that they read. *Read Instantly* has been helping those who everyone else has given up on them!

■ Simple Direct Instruction in *Read Instantly*:

Every lesson begins with easy-to-follow direct instructions for teachers to read and then explain to students. If any students are capable of reading and comprehending these instructions, then they can learn to spell without the help of a teacher.

Teachers may read each comment before a new practice lesson and explain it to students. For instances, teachers may read about the meaning of a concept like "semivowels" and then explain that to students. They may read about the importance of "students reading aloud slowly" and then explain that. They may read a specific "spelling rule" and explain it–students will then read aloud the practice lessons that follow the rules.

In fact, this *Teachers' Guide* is not very necessary because most of the information in it is available inside the books, and each lesson is explicit and self-explanatory. The actual reason we have this guide is to satisfy traditional teachers who insist on having a teachers' edition.

■ **The following Teaching Instructions are a few of many taken from *Read Instantly*:**

Step 1 Follow the order of the lessons presented in this book, as each step is planned carefully and no lesson is placed here arbitrarily. Initially, over 180 spelling patterns, of the various English sounds we call phonics, are placed in a queue awaiting their turn to be introduced logically, one-at-a-time, and in groups of 20 to 50 words.

Step 2 Chapter 1 begins by showing students how each consonant sounds and how it differs from its letter name when used in words. Make the sound of the name of the letter "**h**" (ai+ch), and then tell students that as in "**h**at" the "**h**" sound differs when used in words.

Step 3 At the start, a letter with a sound that is very different from its letter name is avoided. For instance, the "**q**" sounds like a "**k**" and needs to be avoided until it reaches its turn in the queue.

Step 4 Adhere to the **I**nforming **b**efore **I**ntroducing **A**pproach (IBIA) used throughout this book. Most students who have just learned the ABC's expect each letter to sound like its letter name when used in words. For instance, they are unaware that the "**q**" makes a "**k**" sound unless they are informed beforehand and shown enough examples.

Step 5 Pay attention to students with a Logical Learning Style: English was written for memorizers, but logical learners cannot memorize without logical explanations as to why a sound should be spelled one-way and not the other. Students with a logical learning style question why they are told one thing and then asked to read another. They are so logical; they expect to see "My cat is cute." to be "Mi kat iz qut." When words are thrown randomly at people to read, young children who can only learn logically feel the problem with the way English is written but are too young to diagnose the problem. They are not trained linguists and are too young to form all the linguistic questions they wish to ask. If the IBIA is not applied, logical learners will have difficulties in reading or spelling or in both.

Step 6 Avoid using other books that introduce more than one spelling pattern at a time, because that would be like introducing 180 people standing in a queue and then expecting students to remember all of their names. For instance, before asking students to read any words that contain the "**sh**" phonic as in "fi**sh**," you may inform them and then show them how the letter "**s**" combined with the letter "**h**" produce the single sound of "**sh**." You may also justify the use of the "**sh**" by informing them that because English did not have a single letter to represent the sound of "**sh**" the two letters "**s+h**" were combined to represent this sound.

Step 7 The grouping of words of a same sound and spelling pattern is prepared for you in each lesson; simply teach the same words grouped in each lesson.

Step 8 In *Read Instantly*, learners are constantly informed about a change that is about to occur before asking them to read any words that contain such changes. The following examples demonstrate how letters can make sounds different from their letter names, and students need to be gradually informed before introducing each such change:

9

• The "h" sound as in "hot" differs from its sound in "th" as in "mouth."

• The "s" sound as in "rose" and "has" sounds like a "z."

• The "g" sounds like its letter name in "huge," but not in "hug."

• The "a" sounds like its letter name in "main," but not in "man" and not in "auto."

• The "e" sounds like its letter name in "meat," but not in "met" and not in "trailer."

• The "i" sounds like its letter name in "hide," but not in "hid" and not in "skirt."

• The "o" sounds like its letter name in "hope," but not in "hop" and not in "choir."

• The "u" sounds like its letter name in "mute," but not in "mutt" and not in "virus."

• The "c" sounds like its letter name in "cell," like the "k" in "cup," like the "sh" in "social," and like the name of the letter "q" in "cute."

• The "q" always sounds like the letter "k," not like the name of the letter "q" and every "q" is followed by a "u"–students must be informed ahead of time that every "q" is followed by a "u." They also need to be informed that every "qu" is followed by a vowel and that the "qu" sounds like "kw" as in "quit." The sound of the actual letter "q" is not found in "q," but in "cu" as in cute, cucumber, accumulate, cure, secure, etc.

• After informing learners that a letter's name can differ from its sound when used in words, inform them that a single sound can be written in several spelling patterns. For instance, this final sound in these words is spelled in seven different ways, as in fashion, ocean, suspicion, complexion, superstition, expression, and musician. If such endings are presented too soon, they can cause a learner to veer away from learning. A learner may think something is wrong with his or her ability to learn.

• 13 of the 26 English letters change and make sounds that are different from their letter name; it makes no sense to tell learners that the name of this letter is "c" as in "cat" before informing them that the "c" can sound like a "k." Otherwise, they may read "cat" as "sat."

• The following examples are to show the changes in the vowel "a" alone:
[ā: rain, ate, day, able] [ă: fat, fatter] [ɔ: fall, false, auto, law] [a: war] [ə: permanent]

Step 9 Planned Lessons: The steps in which phonics are introduced in *Read Instantly* are not random; lessons are carefully planned and no new letter, sound or spelling pattern is introduced without a warning of its changes beforehand. Hence, anyone capable of learning the alphabet, including dyslexic persons immediately read from this book. They continue to read aloud without a stop, until all the different spelling patterns of all the English sounds are memorized.

Step 10 Read the direct instructions before each lesson and explain that to students. In the beginning, avoid asking students to read any words that contain hard **c**, hard **g**, **s** that sounds like **z**, double letters, **y** as a vowel, consonant blends, digraphs of **h**, two vowels in a word, silent letters, words endings, long words, and begin with one-syllable vowel as presented in this book.

Step 11 Disallow speed-reading before learning to read and spell. Forced speed-reading before learning to read and spell words causes learners to see letters in reverse and then spelling them in reverse. Dyslexia in spelling and in writing letters in reverse ends, after learning to spell and after slowing down to write words slowly.

Step 12 Insist on students reading aloud. Explain to students, from the first day of class, that we acquire information through our five senses and show them how that works. Continue to insist until they read all the practice lessons aloud, whether in or outside of the classroom. If in a classroom, they need to read aloud together in one rhythm.

Step 13 Vowels rule English and they cannot be avoided. Explain that to students and ask them to focus their vision on the vowels when they read. Inform them that learning all the 38 sounds and 96 spelling patterns of vowel is the most important part of learning to read and spell.

Step 14 Warn students that 13 of the 26 letters will be making sounds that are different from their letter names; especially, the five vowels and eight inconsistent consonants. The eight consonants have 50 sounds that are spelled in 60 spelling patterns.

Step 15 Do not force learning and do not stop too long to memorize the spelling of every single word. Learning to spell will be acquired naturally as students keep reading aloud slowly. More spelling rules with detailed practice lessons are in *Learn to Spell 500 Words a Day*, wherein each vowel is isolated in a book.

Step 16 The first four chapters in *Read Instantly* may seem easy for some learners, but Chapters 5 to 9 become gradually sophisticated as each vowel is dissected and isolated in a chapter.

Step 17 Explain all the symbols and concepts used in this book gradually and as needed. For instance, *Italic letters* in this book represent silent letters, like the silent *p* in recei*p*t. However, students do not need to know that until they reach Lesson 6 in Chapter 1 wherein silent letters are introduced.

Step 18 Before asking students to write, ask them to read this entire book aloud slowly. Students must learn to read first before they can begin to write. The steps of language acquisition are speaking, reading, and then writing.

Step 19 When your students finish reading this entire book fluently, they will understand the way English words are structured and will apply their learning to any other words they see.

Step 20 After reading this book fluently, students will do well in schools but will need to learn more words from the rest of the books by Camilia Sadik. In this book for instance, the ea phonic as in meat is presented in 48 words, while all 370 ea words are presented in *The Vowel E*.

11

Book 2: *Learn to Spell 500 Words a Day* (A, E, I, O, U, and Consonants)

Learn to Spell 500 Words a Day is a book in six volumes that are *The Vowel A*, *The Vowel E*, *The Vowel I*, *The Vowel O*, *The Vowel U* and *The Consonants*. Vowels rule English and they cannot be avoided. Hence, each vowel is dissected and isolated in a 152-page colored textbook / workbook, and eight inconsistent consonants are also isolated in a book.

Learn to Spell 500 Words a Day **is for** the intermediate level; it is for those who can read but cannot spell. It is for older children in the 4th grade and up, adult learners, dyslexic persons, and ESL students. From it, intermediate students easily learn the spelling of over 13,000 essential words and gain fluency in reading aloud.

Comprehensive Vowels and Vowels Rules: Every sound and spelling pattern of a vowel is presented in *Learn to Spell 500 Words a Day*. For instance, the five sounds of the vowel "a," which are spelled in 12 spelling patterns are presented in *The Vowel A*. In addition, every lesson begins with a logical explanation or a rule that governs the spelling of vowels. Children in the 4th grade and up and adults apply a spelling rule, read the practice lessons aloud, and learn the spelling of hundreds of words at a time.

Comprehensive Consonants and Consonants Rules: The eight consonants q, x, c, h, g, s, y, and w are inconsistent, and they produce 50 sounds that are spelled in 60 spelling patterns. The 50 sounds and their 60 patterns are presented in *The Consonants*. Every lesson begins with a logical explanation or a rule that governs the spelling of consonants.

All the Prefixes in 900 Words: All the prefixes in 900 words are presented in the last chapter of *The Consonants*.

Comprehensive Phonics-based Spelling Lessons: *Learn to Spell 500 Words a Day* is a comprehensive book of phonics. Its 360 detailed phonics lessons cover over 180 spelling patterns of more than 90 sounds we call phonics. All words of same sound and same spelling pattern, which follow a specific rule, are grouped together and used in multiple practice lessons. For instance, the **i**-*e* phonic as in s**i**t*e* is presented in **450** words, and then the words are used in a nonsensical story about M**i**k*e*.

Each lesson begins with a logical explanation or a spelling rule, followed by nearly all the words that follow that rule, and then most of the words are used in a nonsensical story. Intermediate students are asked to read aloud to learn the spelling of hundreds of words at a time. A sample of a nonsensical story is: D**a**wn took the str**a**w·ber·ries out of the freez·er to let them th**a**w. D**a**wn drank her str**a**w·ber·ry shak*e* with a str**a**w. D**a**wn at*e* r**a**w veg·e·ta·bles and cole·sl**a**w. D**a**wn lik*e*s shrimp and pr**a**wns, etc.

■ **Why *Learn to Spell 500 Words a Day*?**

1. For the Intermediate Level: If you can read but cannot spell the words you read, then *Learn to Spell 500 Words a Day* is the book for you. *Read Instantly* is for beginners, *Learn to Spell 500 Words a Day* is for the intermediate level, and *100 Spelling Rules* is for the advanced level. *Learn to Spell 500 Words a Day* is for children in the 4th grade and up, and for adult learners. Moreover, *Learn to Spell 500 Words a Day* is ideal for K-12 teachers to use as a resource book to teach phonics in 13,000 essential words. Without it, most may not benefit from *100 Spelling Rules*.

2. For Logical Learners: Learners with spelling difficulties learn differently; their learning style is a logical learning style. They need logical explanations or spelling rules before they can memorize the spelling of words. Logical learners, whether children or adults need *Learn to Spell 500 Words a Day* to learn the rules that govern phonics in 13,000 words, which are used in detailed practice lessons.

3. For All Types of Learners: *Learn to Spell 500 Words a Day* works for older children in the 4th grade and up, adult learners, dyslexic persons, and ESL students. Usually, adult learners and older children learn the 13,000 words in *Learn to Spell 500 Words a Day* within weeks or months.

4. For Spelling: After learning the basic words from *Read Instantly*, children and adults need to continue with *Learn to Spell 500 Words a Day* to learn the rest of the words. In *Read Instantly* only a small number of words are introduced, whereas in *Learn to Spell 500 Words a Day* nearly all the words that follow a rule are presented. For instance, the **i**-*e* phonic as in s**i**t*e* is presented in **50** words in *Read Instantly*, but in *Learn to Spell 500 Words a Day* **450** words are presented. In addition, in *Learn to Spell 500 Words a Day* the words are used in a nonsensical story about M**i**k*e*.

5. For Reversing Dyslexia: This is the book that ends dyslexia in spelling and in writing letters in reverse. If anyone was forced into speed-reading before learning to spell words, there is no doubt that person has dyslexia in spelling and in writing letters in reverse. *Learn to Spell 500 Words a Day* is the book to reversing dyslexia or ending it among those who have it. You may read *What is dyslexia?* by Camilia Sadik. Dyslexic learners must slow down to write words slowly for a year or two. In time, they will acquire the ability to speed-read again naturally and without force. Traditional reading programs that advocate speed-reading too soon, give our kids dyslexia before the 3rd grade. Read *How do you get dyslexia?* by Camilia Sadik.

6. For Advanced ESL Students: English language learners who can speak some English and are finished with *Read Instantly*, are ready for *Learn to Spell 500 Words a Day*–they learn phonics similar to the way natives learn phonics.

7. For Guaranteed Learning: *Learn to Spell 500 Words a Day* cannot be avoided. In it lies the core and essence of the English language. Intermediate learners are guaranteed to learn the spelling of 20 to 50 words an hour and to gain fluency and confidence in reading aloud. Dyslexia in spelling and in writing letters in reverse ends, after learning to spell and after slowing down to write words slowly.

About Each Volume in *Learn to Spell 500 Words a Day*

Learn to Spell 500 Words a Day: The Vowel A (vol. 1)

Click to **LOOK INSIDE!**

Vowels rule English and they cannot be avoided and *Learn to Spell 500 Words a Day* is about vowels. The vowel "a" has **five sounds** we call phonics, which are spelled in **12 ways** we call spelling patterns. Every sound and spelling pattern of the vowel "a" is presented *The Vowel A* book, as in these examples: 1. [Short ă: man] 2. [Long ā: may, main, ate, eight, table] 3. [Special sounds of a: fall, false, author, Dawn, warm] 4. [Schwa sound of a: permanent]

The Vowel A contains 65 comprehensive and detailed phonics-based spelling lessons. Each lesson begins with a logical spelling rule, followed by a list of nearly all the words that follow that rule, followed by a nonsensical story that contains most of the listed words, and students are asked to read aloud slowly to memorize the spelling of hundreds of words at a time.

strawberries
Dawn
coleslaw
prawn
raw veggies

Sample of the nonsensical stories to teach the spelling of the same phonic in nearly all the words that contain it:

Dawn took the straw·ber·ries out of the freez·er to let them thaw. Dawn drank her straw·ber·ry shake with a straw. Dawn ate raw veg·e·ta·bles and cole·slaw. Dawn likes shrimp and prawns, etc.

Learn to Spell 500 Words a Day: *The Vowel E* (vol. 2)

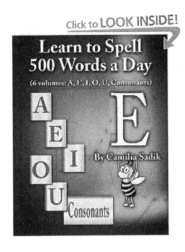

The vowel "e" is dissected and isolated in a volume in the book *Learn to Spell 500 Words a Day.*

The vowel "e" has **seven sounds** we call phonics, which are spelled in **17 ways** we call spelling patterns.

The Vowel E book contains 59 comprehensive and detailed phonics-based spelling lessons. Each lesson begins with a logical spelling rule, followed by a list of nearly all the words that follow that rule, followed by a nonsensical story that contains most of the listed words, and students are asked to read aloud slowly to memorize the spelling of hundreds of words at a time.

Every sound and spelling pattern of the vowel "e" is presented in *The Vowel E,* as in these examples:

1. [Short ĕ: red, bread]

2. [Long ē: meat, meet, Pete, chief, belief, monkey, lucky, he, ski, elite]

3. [Minor sounds of e: enough, eight, break, cake]

4. [Schwa sound of e: poet]

Sample of the nonsensical stories:

The mon·**key**, tur·**key**, and don·**key** drank whis·**key** in Tur·**key**. The mon·**key**, tur·**key**, and don·**key** play*e*d hock·**ey** with the disk jock·**ey** that had a **key** to the zoo. Rick·**ey** laugh*e*d at this ma·lar·**key**. Etc.

Learn to Spell 500 Words a Day: *The Vowel I* (vol. 3)

Click to **LOOK INSIDE!**

The vowel "i" is dissected and isolated in a volume in the book *Learn to Spell 500 Words a Day*.

The vowel "i" has **eight sounds** we call phonics, which are spelled in **19 ways** we call spelling patterns.

The Vowel I contains 62 comprehensive and detailed phonics-based spelling lessons. Each lesson begins with a logical spelling rule, followed by a list of nearly all the words that follow that rule, followed by a nonsensical story that contains most of the listed words, and then students are asked to read aloud slowly to memorize the spelling of hundreds of words at a time.

Every sound and spelling pattern of the vowel "i" is presented in *The Vowel I*, as in these examples:

1. [Short ĭ: Jim, gym]

2. [Long ī: night, sign, child, die, dye, type, icon, by, bypass]

3. [Minor sounds of i: bikini, onion, mission, vision, soldier]

4. [Schwa sound of i: credible, analyst]

Sample of the nonsensical stories (y-*e* = ī-*e*):

burning pyre

thyme

acolyte

type

Lyle has a nice style. Lyle takes en·zymes mixed with thyme. Lyle types 90 WPM. Lyle needs to an·a·lyze be·fore he can mem·o·rize. Lyle and Kyle's names rhyme. Lyle and Kyle do not ste·re·o·type peo·ple. Kyle cares for a tyke–par·a·lyzed dog. Etc.

16

Learn to Spell 500 Words a Day: *The Vowel O* (vol. 4)

Click to **LOOK INSIDE!**

The vowel "o" is dissected and isolated in a volume in the book *Learn to Spell 500 Words a Day*.

The vowel "o" has **12 sounds** we call phonics, which are spelled in **20 ways** we call spelling patterns.

The Vowel O contains 76 comprehensive and detailed phonics-based spelling lessons. Each lesson begins with a logical spelling rule, followed by a list of nearly all the words that follow that rule, followed by a nonsensical story that contains most of the listed words, and students are asked to read aloud slowly to memorize the spelling of hundreds of words at a time.

Every sound and spelling pattern of the vowel "o" is presented in *The Vowel O*, as in these examples:

1. [Short ŏ: hop]

2. [Long ō: tow, toe, soul, loan, hope, so, cold, boy, boil]

3. [Nine other sounds of o: cow, counselor, cool, good, bought, do, you, choir, touch]

4. [Schwa sound of o: memory]

Sample of the nonsensical stories:

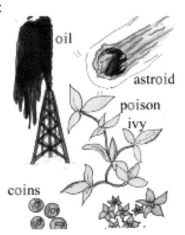

oil
astroid
poison
ivy
coins

The man from Det·roit had to toil and moil to find some oil un·der the soil. The man from Det·roit went to Il·li·nois to search for oil wells. The man from Det·roit missed his ap·point·ment be·cause of the tur·moil. Etc.

Learn to Spell 500 Words a Day: *The Vowel U* (vol. 5)

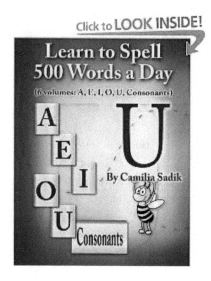

The vowel "u" is dissected and isolated in a volume in the book *Learn to Spell 500 Words a Day*.

The vowel "u" has **six sounds** we call phonics, which are spelled in **28 ways** we call spelling patterns.

The Vowel U contains 45 comprehensive and detailed phonics-based spelling lessons. Each lesson begins with a logical spelling rule, followed by a list of nearly all the words that follow that rule, followed by a nonsensical story that contains most of the listed words, and students are asked to read aloud slowly to memorize the spelling of hundreds of words at a time.

Every sound and spelling pattern of the vowel "u" is presented in *The Vowel U*, as in these examples:

1. [Short ŭ: dug, Doug, flood, ton, done]

2. [Long ū: sue, suit, feud, few, cute, menu, soup, shoo, shoe, tomb, to, prove]

3. [Special sounds of u: out, language, guest, curb]

4. [Schwa sound of u: stadium, humorous, nature]

Sample of the nonsensical stories (**double u = uu**):

jewelry
screwdriver
screws
newspaper

Math·ew grew up in a brand-new house. Math·ew's dad used to re·view Math·ew's home·work. Math·ew went on a crew with his neph·ew and a few friends. Math·ew *k*new his new cur·few time. Math·ew *k*new some Heb·rew. Etc.

Learn to Spell 500 Words a Day: *The Consonants* (vol. 6)

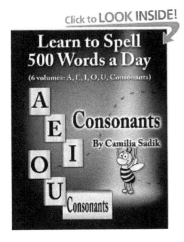

Eight inconsistent consonants are dissected and isolated in a volume in the *Learn to Spell 500 Words a Day*. The eight inconsistent consonants c, g, h, q, s, x, w, and y produce 50 sounds we call phonics, which are spelled in 60 ways we call spelling patterns. In addition, all of the prefixes in 900 words are presented in the last chapter of *The Consonants*.

The Consonants contains 45 comprehensive and detailed phonics-based spelling lessons. Each lesson begins with a logical spelling rule, followed by a list of nearly all the words that follow that rule, and students are asked to read aloud slowly to memorize the spelling of hundreds of words at a time.

Every sound and spelling pattern of the eight inconsistent consonants is presented in *The Consonants* and students are informed beforehand of any inconsistency that is about to occur.

Summary of a Lesson from *The Consonants*

Rule: The letter **K** is not allowed in long words and it occurs in a very limited number of words (approximately 40 useful words).

When you hear yourself saying the **K** sound that is not followed by a "u" sound as in "queen" or by an "s" sound as is "tax," spell that **K** sound with a **C**, not a **K** 98% of the time. Specifically, spell the **K** sound with a **C** in these 12 spelling patterns:

1. [cat, academy]

2. [cold, consonants]

3. [cup, accurate]

4. [club, conclude]

5. [crop, describe]

6. [fact, character]

7. [sick, fantastic]

8. [accident, back]

9. [sock, occupy]

10. [deck, eccentric]

11. [luck, chuckle]

12. [choir, chemistry]

Book 3: *100 Spelling Rules* (Rules followed by lists of words that follow them)

100 Spelling Rules is for the Advanced Level

Advanced students are those who finished learning from *Learn to Spell 500 Words a Day*, which is for the intermediate level. These 100 spelling rules discovered by Linguist Camilia Sadik have made spelling logical and possible for all ages and all types of learners.

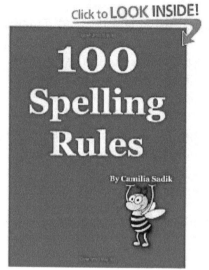

100 Spelling Rules is a 250-page colored book by Linguist Camilia Sadik who spent 15 years intensely dissecting English. Each lesson begins with a spelling rule; each rule is followed by a list of nearly all the words that follow it, and advanced students are guaranteed to learn the spelling of 20 to 50 long words an hour.

Advanced Level: Advanced students are those who finished learning the 13,000 essential words from *Learn to Spell 500 Words a Day*. Most of the rules in this book are about suffixes or word endings. The rules that govern the spelling of vowels inside words are in *Learn to Spell 500 Words a Day*.

These Books are Cumulative: Vowels rule English and they cannot be avoided. Without the practice lessons, in the vowels books, *100 Spelling Rules* may teach the rules but not the actual spelling of words. Learning to spell requires learning the rules when they are applied in phonics-based spelling lessons; it does not mean learning the rules alone. Moreover, one needs to be fluent in spelling a word like "sign" before spelling "consignment." Pay attention to the title of *Learn to Spell 500 Words a Day*; the title says this is the book to learn to spell, not *100 Spelling Rules*. In addition, more than 100 spelling rules are applied throughout all of Sadik's phonics books.

Comprehensive Spelling Rules: *100 Spelling Rules* is a comprehensive book of the rules that govern phonics and word endings. Its 105 detailed spelling lessons cover nearly all the questions that can be asked about spelling an English sound one-way and not the other. Moreover, all words of same sound and same spelling pattern, which follow a specific rule, are grouped together and prepared for students to read aloud and learn. For instance, the -sion phonic as in expression is presented in all 47 words that contain this phonic.

■ **Why *100 Spelling Rules*?**

1. For the Advanced Level: If you can read and spell but still need to improve your spelling, then *100 Spelling Rules* is the book for you. *Read Instantly* is for beginners, *Learn to Spell 500 Words a Day* is for the intermediate level, and *100 Spelling Rules* is for the advanced level. *100 Spelling Rules* is for children in the 4th grade and up, and for adult learners. Moreover, *100*

Spelling Rules is ideal for teachers to teach the spelling of hundreds of words at time to advanced students or to use as a resource book.

2. For Logical Learners: Learners with spelling difficulties learn differently; their learning style is a logical learning style. They need logical explanations or spelling rules before they can memorize the spelling of words. Logical learners, whether children or adults need *100 Spelling Rules* to learn the spelling of 12,000 long, multi-syllabic words.

3. For All Types of Learners: *100 Spelling Rules* works for older children in the 4th grade and up, adult learners, dyslexic persons, and advanced ESL students.

4. For Spelling: After learning phonics in 1,400 basic words from *Read Instantly*, children and adults need to continue with learning phonics from *Learn to Spell 500 Words a Day* in 13,000 essential words. After that, they need to continue with learning phonics from *100 Spelling Rules* in 12,000 long, multi-syllabic words.

5. For Advanced ESL Students: English language learners who can speak English and are finished with *Read Instantly* and with *Learn to Spell 500 Words a Day*, are now ready for *100 Spelling Rules*–they learn similar to the way natives learn.

6. For Guaranteed Learning: *100 Spelling Rules* cannot be avoided because it contains 12,000 significantly useful words that must be learned. Advanced learners are guaranteed to learn logically the spelling of 20 to 50 words an hour and gain fluency and confidence in reading aloud. Dyslexia in spelling and in writing letters in reverse ends, after learning to spell and after slowing down to write words slowly.

Book 4: The Compound Words (7,000 Compound & Hyphenated Words)

The Compound Words

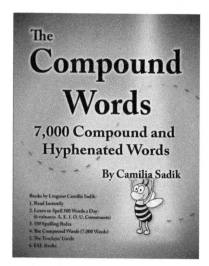

The Compound Words by Camilia Sadik is a 152-page colored textbook and workbook. It is the ninth book in a series of ten. With the help of a teacher, *The Compound Word* can be for children of any age. It is also for adults and older children who can read but cannot spell the words that they read. *The Compound Words* contains over **5,000** compound words and **2,000** hyphenated words.

Grouped Words: The 7,000 words are isolated in this 152-page book, grouped alphabetically, colored, and prepared for adults and children to read and learn.

For instance, 106 compound words and 29 hyphenated words that begin with an "a" are grouped, colored, and listed on the first three pages in *The Compound Words.* The words are grouped and prepared for teachers to teach and / or for students to learn.

A compound word is composed of two or more words, as in cannot. **A hyphenated word is** made of the two or more words, which are separated by hyphens, as in face-to-face.

Learning the compound words is fun and easy. You will learn the spelling of hundreds of words at a time, simply by looking at these words. If anyone wishes to memorize the 7,000 words in a very short time, they need to read them aloud slowly as many times as needed until all words are memorized.

Book 5: How to Teach Phonics - Teachers' Guide

How to Teach Phonics - Teachers' Guide **is this book you are reading.** It contains easy instructions for how to use the 10 phonics-based reading and spelling books by Camilia Sadik. It contains comprehensive spelling tests; and the words in the test are carefully selected to include nearly all the spelling pattern of phonics. In it are explanations of old and new concepts like vowels, long vowels, short vowels, semivowels, schwa, syllables, phonics, dyslexia, dyslexia in spelling, dyslexia in writing letters in reverse, ending dyslexia, preventing dyslexia before the 4th grade, logical learning style, etc.

In the *Teachers Guide* are explanations of the symbols and concepts used in the books, of the 30 unique learning features used, and of the teaching methodology used.

3 The 30 Unique Learning Features in Camilia Sadik's Books

The 30 Unique Learning Features in One Comprehensive Program

All learners capable of learning the English alphabet can now read and master spelling–they do that not in year but in months, weeks, and sometimes days. The value of this phonics-based reading and spelling program is in its entirety. Using this program, one day is equivalent to a year of learning in a traditional learning institution. All ages and all types of learners are guaranteed to learn the spelling of hundreds of words at a time. The 30 learning features are:

1 Every word is divided into **syllables:** win·dow

2 All the **silent** letters are **italicized:** su*b*·p*o*e·na

3 Every phonic to be learned is **bolded** and **colored:** ran, rain, etc.

4 All the practice lessons are in a **large font size:** rain, main, cam·paign, etc.

5 **100 spelling rules:** Applying the 100 newly discovered rules in every book, students understand when to spell a sound one-way and not the other.

✓**Sample rule:** We usually use "cial" after a vowel as in "so·cial," and "tial" after a consonant as in "substantial."

✓**Sample rule:** We usually use "ance" after a full word that can standalone and has a meaning as in "attendance," and we use "ence" after a non-word as in "evidence."

Logical Learners need Logic before Memorizing: The reason logical learners, especially dyslexic persons, quickly learn to read and spell from this program is that they are good thinkers, and good thinkers need logical answers to their questions before they can memorize the spelling of words. Their learning style is a logical learning style.

6 **Grouping of words that share similar sounds and spelling patterns:** All words that share the same sound and spelling pattern, which follow a specific spelling rule are grouped together to be read aloud and memorized. For instance, the endings "ance" and "ence" occur in approximately **131** words, and they are all grouped in a list and made ready for the learners to read aloud and learn. Similarly, the "ai" phonic as in rain, main, mail, straight, proclaim, etc. is in approximately **210** words, and all the "ai" words are grouped together and listed on a few pages.

When they see such lists, learners are no longer intimidated by learning to read or spell. They feel they can conquer English instead of letting it conquer them. After seeing these types of wordlists, students express the feelings of relief, and here are some of their comments:

"All these years I didn't know that." "Is this all the words?" "Just 210 words, that's easy."

"My teachers said to look up words in the dictionary, but the dictionary wasn't like this."

"Do you mean if I learn these words, I won't have to worry about looking for more 'ai' words?"

An inmate in Missouri said, "Man, I can use all these words in a letter." He said that as if these 210 words were not accessible to him before and that now they were his to use.

7 Every vowel is isolated in a book: Because vowels are inconsistent and each vowel sound has many spelling patterns, an entire book is used to teach all the sounds and spelling patterns of each vowel. Nearly all the words that share a specific sound and spelling pattern are listed and handed to students to read aloud and learn. We need not ask students to do the grouping of words, because that will require ten or more years of hard work plus the skills of a good linguist. A student should not have to become a linguist in order to read or spell. The grouping process begins by isolating each vowel in a book. For instance, the five sounds of the vowel "a" that are spelled in 12 spelling patterns are presented in *The Vowel A.*

8 Each vowel sound is presented in a section in the book: Every vowel has a number of sounds–each sound is presented in a section in the book. For instance, the vowel "a" has five major sounds and each sound is presented in a section in *The Vowel A.*

9 The fiver sounds of "a" are spelled in 12 spelling patterns: Every spelling pattern of a sound is presented in a chapter in the book. The first sound of "a" is the long "a" sound and it is spelled in five ways. Each way is then presented in a chapter.

10 Example of a section in the book: Section 1: The long ā sound spelled in five ways, as in rain, cake, day, table, and eight.

11 Every spelling pattern of each sound of a vowel is then isolated in a chapter: Chapter 1: The "ai" phonic is the first spelling pattern of the long ā sound.

12 Every spelling pattern of each sound is justified by a rule that governs phonics: Example: As in ta´·ble, the "a" at the end of a stressed syllable sounds long, just like the name of the letter A.

13 Nearly all words that share the same phonic or follow a specific spelling rule are listed: Lists of words are presented right after explaining the rule; words are prepared for students to read aloud and learn. For examples, the "ai" as in "rain" is in a list of 210 words, the "a-*e*" as in "cak*e*" is in a list of 414 words, the "ay" as in "day" is in a list of 24 words, the "a'" as in "ta´·ble" is in a countless number of words, the "ei" as in "eight" is in a list of 27 words.

14 Most of the words on the list are used in a nonsensical story like this: Most of the 413 "a-*e*" words are used in a story about "Jak*e*," as in: Jak*e* bak*e*s his own cak*e*. Jak*e* eats the cak*e* when he wak*e*s. Jak*e* drinks milk·shak*e* with his cak*e*. Jak*e* mak*e*s his pet snak*e*s eat cak*e*. Jak*e* tak*e*s the cak*e* to the lak*e*. Jak*e* rak*e*s his own lawn. Jak*e* had to fix his car's brak*e*s. Etc.

15 There is, at least, one illustration taken from the story, like these two:

16 **Comparison as in plain and plane:** At the end of a section, there are comparisons among different spelling patterns of the same sound, which are presented like this: In the previous stories, El*ai*ne was the one who at*e* **plain** yo·gurt. Jak*e* was the one who had an air·**plane**. Etc.

17 **The eight inconsistent consonants c, g, h, q, s, x, w, and y are isolated in a book:** In addition to the five books of vowels, eight inconsistent consonants are also dissected and isolated in a book. The eight consonants produce 50 sounds that are spelled in 60 spelling patterns. There are rules too that govern the spelling of consonants. Unlike the popular rule which states that the hard "c" is spelled in ca, co, and cu. It is specified in this book that the hard "c" is spelled in the 12 spelling patterns, as in cat, cold, cute, clever, crown, fact, logic, account, occupy, eccentric, chuckle, and chemistry. Enough examples follow each pattern and all the logical reasons for when to spell the hard "c" one-way and not the other are presented–logical reasons are also given to learn when to spell with a hard "c" or with a hard "ch" as in "chemistry."

18 **The Students Reading Aloud Approach (S-RAA):** After the words are listed, students are asked to apply the S-RAA that Sadik developed and class-tested over the years. The S-RAA means that it is not the teachers nor the parents that need to read aloud for the students, but the students need to read aloud. They need to read the lists of words and then the stories that these words are used. Using the S-RAA causes students to memorize the spelling of words naturally through senses and without forced memorizations.

19 **The Reading Slowly Approach:** This approach gives students enough time to see the way words are spelled. It also helps them slow down to avoid seeing and then writing letters in reverse. Adults who were told in the past they needed to hurry to keep up with schoolwork, felt forced to speed-read and ended up seeing letters in reverse. With this program, they know it's okay to take the time needed while learning to spell–their self-esteem rises drastically when their teacher asks them to slow down because they are reading too fast.

20 **New concepts are introduces:** Linguist Camilia Sadik introduces new concepts into the English language; and sometimes she alienates an existing concept from its traditional meaning and grants it a new meaning.

For instance, "learning phonics" is traditionally said to be learning English sounds. However, saying that is not enough because learning phonics now means learning all the various spelling patterns of all the English sounds in nearly all the words that contain them. We do not only teach the sound but also the spelling patterns of each sound, as in the final sound in fa*shion*, o*cean*, suspi*cion*, comple*xion*, supersti*tion*, expre*ssion*, and musi*cian*.

The 26 English letters produce over 90 sounds we call phonics, which are spelled in approximately 180 ways we call spelling patterns. We are not only interested in learning the sounds but also in learning the various spelling patterns of each sound in 32,000 words or more.

Another instance is that the letters **l**, **m**, **n**, **r**, and **s** are now called semivowels. The author alienated the word "semivowels" from its traditional meaning and named the consonants l, m, n, r, and s "semivowels."

Unlike the rest of the consonants, the semivowels have some sounds of their own and they can have various effects on the vowels that precede them. See how the semivowels can make the vowels that precede them long in words, as in c**o**ld, c**o**m*b*, n**i**nth, p**o**rt, and diabet**e**s.

Words labeled as "sight words" are now explained by this *Semivowels Theory*. It turns out that the so-called "sight words" are governed by spelling rules too. See lesson 71 in *100 Spelling Rules* for the complete *Semivowels Theory*.

21 **Diagnosing the problem with English spelling:** Only in this program are we able to diagnose the problem associated with why people cannot spell. A quick simple answer for that is that a single English sound can be spelled in a number of ways. Learners may read such sounds, but may not always remember which spelling pattern to choose. For instance, they may not remember which of these 10 spelling patterns to choose when they hear the single sound of long ē, as in t**ea**, fr**ee**, concr**e**t*e*, ch**ie**f, prot**ei**n, cit**y**, chimn**ey**, L**e**o, fianc**é**, and submarin*e*.

22 **Preventing or ending dyslexia:** Millions of dollars are being spent on dyslexia and no one else claims to come up with answers to what causes it, how to prevent it, or how to end it. Classic descriptions of dyslexia are that it is innate and that it is a learning disability that cannot be prevented or reversed. Only in Camilia Sadik's program is the mystery of dyslexia uncovered. Sadik offers concrete solutions to preventing or ending dyslexia. Dyslexia is given to kids before the 4th grade, and it can be easily prevented if the *Informing before Introducing* principle is applied. Details about this principle are in *Read Instantly*. Sadik spent years to prepare a simple program for students, with or without dyslexia, to read the practice lessons aloud slowly and learn the spelling of hundreds of words at a time.

23 **The only comprehensive phonics program:** Traditional programs that teach phonics offer only bits and pieces of scattered phonics. This is the only comprehensive phonics program. In it are all of the sounds we call phonics and their various spelling patterns. Traditionally, teaching phonics means teaching the sounds, not all the spelling patterns of sounds and not in that many words. They may teach the long ē sound in a few words, as in sp**ea**k, g**ee**k, b**ea**k, un**i**que, w**ea**k, Gr**ee**k, etc.

No other known program groups nearly all of the words that share similar sound and spelling pattern. Instead, they often mix up words of the same sound but different spelling patterns and expect students to learn and memorize. Mixing of words like sp**ea**k, g**ee**k, b**ea**k, un**i**que, w**ea**k, Gr**ee**k, etc. without any logical structure overwhelms students and veers them away from learning. Students become hopeless when trying to figure out when to spell the same long ē sound one-way and not the other.

24 **The 26 English letters should have been 206 letters:** The ABC's should have been [26 letters + 180 spelling patterns of sounds we call phonics = 206]. Phonics and all of the spelling patterns of phonics are presented logically in this program.

Teachers please, do not stop after teaching the ABC's. Every spelling pattern of a sound must be taught immediately after teaching the 26 letters and before asking students to read words in stories.

We cannot teach the letter "s" and the letter "h" independently and leave out the phonic "sh" as in "**sh**ip." In addition, we need to offer logical reasons to explain the use of "sh." In this case, we tell students that the 26 letters don't have a single letter to represent the "sh" sound, and that we have had to combine two letters to write this sound.

Also, try to introduce the "sh" in a number of words until it is learned. Only after teaching each of the 180 patterns of phonics, should we be asking students to read words in sentences and stories. Again, teaching phonics is like teaching the rest of the ABC's.

25 **Nearly all the prefixes in 900 words:** The prefixes are presented in 900 words in last chapter of *The Consonants*. This is a summary of a sample lesson:
✓ bio = of life or living: bi·o·chem·is·try, bi·o·de·grad·a·ble, bi·ol·o·gy, etc.
✓ geo = of earth: ge·ol·o·gy, ge·og·ra·phy, ge·om·e·try, etc.

26 **Nearly all the silent letters are isolates in a chapter:** In addition to making silent letters italic throughout this entire program, a list of nearly all the silent letters in **384** words is presented in a Lesson 65 in the *100 Spelling Rules*, as in the following examples:
✓ The **15** words that contain a silent *b* are:
com*b*, bom*b*, bom*b*·ing, lam*b*, num*b*, thum*b*, crum*b*, dum*b*, dum*b*·er, plum*b*·er, clim*b*, dou*b*t, de*b*t, tom*b*, and su*b*·poe·na

27 **7,000 compound and hyphenated words are isolated in a book:**
back·ache*e*, back·bon*e*, back·sid*e*, back·stag*e*, back·yard, back·ground, etc.
back-load, back-pedal, back-and-forth, back-to-back, etc.

28 **The order of introducing each phonic in *Read Instantly* is carefully planned.** Initially, all of the spelling patterns of phonics are placed in a queue and then introduced logically, one-at-a-time and in a group of 20 to 50 words.

Beginners are informed before introducing a new pattern of a sound. Hence, anyone, capable of learning the ABC's learns to read, without exceptions. Learners labeled as "impossible cases" immediately read aloud from this book. Most finished reading it in days or hours.

✓**Example: q** says **k** and **cu** says **q**

There can be a difference between the name of a letter and its actual sound when used in words. For instance, the letter "q" used in the word "queen" sounds like the "k" sound, but the name of the letter "q" is found in "cu" as in "cute."

Without explaining, students who have just learned the 26 letters expect each letter to sound like its letter name when used in words; they do not know that the "q" makes a "k" sound unless they are informed of this fact beforehand. Therefore, before asking students to read any words that contain "q," inform them the sound of "q" when used in words is a "k" sound.

If they are not informed of such changes, students may always have difficulties reading or spelling words that contain "q" and they may end up spelling "frequently" as "frekwently" and "cucumber" as "qucumber."

Analytic learners tend to wonder why they are told one thing and then asked to read or write something else. Young children are not linguists and cannot diagnose the problem with English spelling–they are incapable of forming all the linguistic questions they need to ask. Before they know it, they are diagnosed with dyslexia.

29 **Dissecting English sounds, letters & words:** Students' feelings do count and they need to feel in control when using their first language. For instance, isolating the vowel "a" in a book and stating the fact that the vowel "a" has five sounds makes them wish to learn more.

Moreover, learning that the five sounds of the vowel "a" are spelled in 12 ways makes them feel more in control over their own language.

Imagine how they would feel after they read all the specifics sounds and spelling patterns of the "a" and then use each of the five sounds and each of the 12 spelling patterns in practice lessons in 2,200 words! In this specific case of the vowel "a," they learn that the vowel "a" has five major sounds, which are spelled in these 12 ways in this order:

ā: rain, ray, ate, eight, table

ă: fat, fatter

ɔ: fall, false, auto, law

a: war

ə: permanent

Depending on what follows the "a," it can sound long, short, like the "au" in "auction," or like a schwa as in "separate." We need to slow down to see what comes after the vowel "a" before reading it.

30 **A Combination of formulas in one program makes learning inescapable:** Linguist Camilia Sadik spent 15 years intensely dissecting English and preparing a breakthrough program for students to read and learn the spelling of hundreds of words at a time. The magnitude of Sadik's program is in its entirety. Encompassing that many unique learning features in one program makes learning inescapable for all ages and all types of learners. If any student does not learn from one feature, he or she may learn from the rest of the features.

The ēy occurs in approximately 40 nouns and after k, l, and one n.

-key Mic·key is a zoo·keeper and he has a key to the zoo. Mic·key used to be a disk jock·ey, and he played some mu·sic at the zoo. The mon·key, don·key, and tur·key drank whis·key. The mon·key, don·key, and tur·key played hock·ey. Rick·ey laughed when he heard a·bout this ma·lar·key. Rick·ey, Mick·ey's friend, is a jock·ey at the race·track.

turkey

hockey

donkey

monkey

key

volleyball

barley soup

parsley

-ley Shir·ley, Hen·ley, and Kel·ley live in the val·ley. They play volley·ball in the al·ley near the trol·ley. Shir·ley likes pars·ley in her beef bar·ley soup. Kel·ley goes to Ber·ke·ley u·ni·ver·si·ty.

-ney Rod·ney's kid·ney is in·fect·ed from chim·ney smoke. Rod·ney went on a jour·ney a·way from that chim·ney. Rod·ney saw Dis·ney·land. Rod·ney's jour·ney made his kid·ney feel bet·ter. Rod·ney's at·tor·ney said that mon·ey is hon·ey.

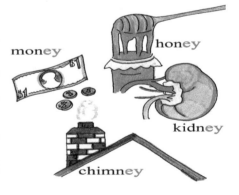

money

honey

kidney

chimney

Who are these books for?

■ **All Ages and All Levels Benefit:** Briefly, these phonics-based reading and spelling books are cumulative and all benefit from them. They are for all ages and all types of learners. Specifically, they are for older children from the 4th grade and up, for teachers and parents of younger children in K-3, for teachers of K-12, for adults from diverse backgrounds, and for ESL students.

■ **For Logical Learners:** The learning style of persons with spelling difficulties is a logical learning style; they require logical explanations before they can memorize the spelling of words. Logical learners need to know when to spell a sound one-way and not the other, as in the final sound in fashion, ocean, suspicion, complexion, superstition, depression, and electrician. Linguist Camilia Sadik spent 15 years discovering over 100 spelling rules, applying the rules in 600 phonics lessons, and preparing 10 very logical spelling books.

■ **For Older Children and Adults as Self-help Books:** Usually, it is too late for adults and older children in the 4th grade and up, to memorize the spelling of words, without first understanding the rules that govern phonics. Now, they have the phonics' opportunity step-by-step–they quickly learn to spell over 32,000 words with or without the help of a teacher.

■ **For Dyslexic Persons:** Dyslexia in spelling and in writing letters in reverse ends after learning to spell and after slowing down to write words slowly. All of those diagnosed with dyslexia, with no exceptions, learned and overcame their reading and spelling difficulties.

■ **For Teachers and Parents of K-3:** The book *Read Instantly* is ideal for younger children in K-3 who need the help of their teachers or parents.

■ **For Teachers and Parents of K-12:** These 10 workbooks and resource books are prepared for teachers to teach the spelling of hundred of words at a time.

Parents must get involved because teaching the spelling of phonics in thousands of words is a process that requires much more time than simply teaching the ABC's. Obviously, our schools have not been able to do it alone; otherwise, we wouldn't have had such high illiteracy rate. No teacher has the time needed to teach your child to read or spell over 180 spelling patterns of 90 sounds in thousands of words. Teachers may recommend these books to parents, and most parents will be more than happy to get involved.

■ **For ESL Learners:** All ages of ESL learners benefit from Camilia Sadik's books. In the beginning, they benefit from the two books *Read Instantly* and *English for Nonnative English Speakers*. At a later stage, they benefit from the rest of the books just as much as native-English speakers do. ESL learners learn to read phonics from *Read Instantly* even if they cannot speak

English. Learning to read phonics is like learning to read the ABC's—similar to the way they learn to read the letter "m" as in "map," they can learn to read the phonic "tion" as in "nation." We teach ESL learners to read letters, which do not have meaning. Learning to read a sound like "tion" is the same as learning to read the letter "m" and the "m" does not have a meaning.

■ **For All Types of Learners:** Because of the number of ways each English sound is spelled, no one is expected to be a perfect speller. The vast majority of people have some difficulties in spelling, including memorizers. In fact, most memorizers complain from misspelling the schwa sound. Some complain from not knowing when to double the consonant in the middle of certain long words like doubling the "r" in "tomorrow" or the "t" in "committed" or from not doubling the "t" in "limited." There are logical answers to both of these questions in *100 Spelling Rules*.

■ **For Dyslexia Prevention before the 3rd Grade:** Using *Read Instantly*, dyslexia in reading or spelling can be prevented before the 3rd grade. Moreover, anyone from any age group who knows the ABC's is guaranteed to learn to read this 152-page book fluently. To learn how to prevent dyslexia, please read *How do you get dyslexia* by Camilia Sadik.

■ **For ADD that is caused by Dyslexia:** Students diagnosed with Attention Deficient Disorder (ADD) that is caused by dyslexia learned and overcame their reading and spelling difficulties. Not only did they learn to read and spell; but also, they learned to pay attention and proved they can focus highly on one subject at a time.

■ **For ADD Prevention:** The vast majority of children who are diagnosed with ADD cannot spell and some cannot read at all. Their learning style is a logical learning style and they have proven to learn to read and spell quicker than any other students.

Typically, their first reaction is that they had given up on learning from all the traditional programs presented to them. Traditional programs veer them away from learning. As soon as they change their attitude, they begin to pour a tremendous amount of energy into their learning process–their high energy is so easily transformed from negative into positive energy. Not only do they learn to read and spell, but they calm down and score A's in other classes.

■ **For Alzheimer's Prevention:** A number of elderly persons have proven to relearn the spelling of hundreds of words at a time, and that caused them to restore a big portion of their memory. Elderly persons who spend a long time without speaking to anyone read aloud not only to remember to spell but to speak as well–reading aloud is the closest act to speaking.

■ **For All Ages, All Levels, and All Types of Learners:** These books are not limited to persons with dyslexia or ADD. They are not limited to ESL students or to logical learners. All benefit from these comprehensive phonics-based reading and spelling books, and they are for all types of learners. Specifically, they are for adults from diverse backgrounds, for older children from the 4th grade and up, for teachers and parents of younger children in K-3, for teachers of K-12, and for ESL students.

1. How to teach or tutor from *Read Instantly* by Camilia Sadik

Students need Understand Why Vowels Must be Taken Seriously

1. Vowels are the strong letters because vowels have sounds, while consonants like the "t" are soundless unless they are paired with a vowel–vowels are responsible for the sounds we make in our speech.

2. Vowels are very inconsistent–each vowel has five or more sounds we call phonics and every sound is spelled in 12 or more ways we call spelling patterns. Because vowels are very inconsistent, they can be very difficult to learn and it is critical to learn how vowels change.

3. Vowels rule English and they cannot be avoided. Hence, learners, whether children or adults, need to be informed that vowels are more important than the consonants.

4. The most basic rule of vowels is that vowels help each other, and learners need to keep that in mind until they see how this will be applied in future lessons. Teachers need to keep in mind that the first rule of vowels is that when two vowels are walking, the first one does the talking, as in main, meat, tie, boat, and argue. The second rule of vowels is that two vowels can still walk when there is only one consonant between them, as in late, theme, dine, hope, and cute. Because consonants are the weak letters, in a syllable, one consonant between two vowels is too weak to keep the two vowels from helping each other. This explains seeing so many double consonants in words, as in latter, messed, dinner, hopped, and rubbed.

■ **Placing Phonics in a Queue:** In *Read Instantly*, all phonics are initially placed in a queue awaiting their turn to be introduced logically, one-at-time, and in a group of 20 to 50 words. The principle used throughout *Read Instantly* is the *Informing before Introducing* principle that was developed and class-tested by Linguist Camilia Sadik. For instance, learners are not asked to read a word like "is" before informing them ahead of time that the "s" can sound like a "z" at the end of certain one-syllable words as in is, as, has, was, bags, beds, loves, etc. Every step in *Read Instantly* is carefully planned and no phonic or word is randomly thrown at people to read or spell. Every lesson begins by informing learners about a new phonic that is about to be introduced.

■ **The Order of Presenting Phonics in *Read Instantly*:** The order of presenting phonics in *Read Instantly* is most suitable for learners with a logical learning style. It is unlike traditional programs that throw sentences randomly at kids and then expect them to read and memorize the spelling of the words in these sentences. The author assumes that all learners had just learned the 26 English letters, and are ready to learn phonics in words and that learning phonics is like learning the rest of the ABC's. Every phonic is presented individually after awaiting its turn to be introduced, it is then explained and justified by a logical spelling rule, and then presented in 10 to 20 simple words. No student is asked to read any words that contain a phonic that has not yet been introduced. For instance, the author avoids introducing a word like "i**nn**" that contains double letters until informing learners that double letters exist in English and that they exist for various useful reasons–the "**nn**" in "i**nn**" is to tell it apart from "i**n**," for instance. Only after informing and justifying, are learners asked to read words that contain double letters.

■ **Presenting Consonants:** In the beginning, no inconsistent consonant is introduced. For instance, a word like "m**y**" is avoided because students are not yet informed that the consonant "y" can sound like an "i." Instead, the "y" is first introduced as a consonant in words like **y**es, and **y**am. The "qu" is also avoided because it sounds like a "kw." Describe the difference between a letter's name and its sound when used in words; it is similar to the name of a telephone and the sound a telephone makes when it rings. There are eight inconsistent consonants in English but their inconsistency is less drastic than the inconsistency in vowels. For this reason, each vowel is isolated in a book but the eight consonants together are isolated in a book. The eight inconsistent consonants produce 50 sounds that are spelled in 60 spelling patterns.

■ **Presenting Vowels:** Only one sound of each vowel is first introduced; namely, the short vowel sounds are first introduced in small one-syllable words. For instance, only words like m**a**d, m**e**d, m**i**d, m**o**d, and m**u**d are initially introduced. The author avoids presenting long vowels and any other sounds or spelling patterns of vowels until a sound reaches its turn in the queue. Tutors please enunciate the vowel sounds loud and clear and ask students to do the same—imagine yourself downstairs calling "M**o**m!" who is upstairs and cannot easily hear you.

■ **Presenting More Consonants:** The principal of *Informing before Introducing* continues while learning the short vowels. For instance, students are first informed that there are silent letters in English and that silent letters can have useful functions–after that, they are asked to read aloud these words that contain silent letters, which are *italicized* in the book like this:

*k*not	*k*nob	*k*nit	lo*dg*e	dum*b*	bom*b*

■ **Why Informing before Introducing?** Why do we need to wait before introducing an inconsistent letter that does not sound like its letter name? Why should we avoid introducing words like **c**at, **ch**ip, ba**g**, happ**y**, **au**to, ro**s**e, l**ow**, a**dd**, etc.? The reason for avoiding the introduction of such letters is that people deserve to be informed that the "c" can sound like a "k," the "ch" is a single special sound, the "g" has a hard sound, the "y" at the end of long words can sound like the vowel "e," the "au" is a single special sound, the "s" can sound like a "z" when between two vowels, and the "ow" can sound like an "o." They deserve to know that double letters exist before they are asked to read words with double letters; they need to be informed that silent letters exist before asking them to read the silent "b" in words like "bom*b*," etc. These are only a few examples to show how each phonic is presented in this book.

■ **Dyslexic Persons need to Crawl before They can Run:** In *Read Instantly*, there are more than 180 spelling patterns of over 90 sounds we call phonics placed in a queue and learned one-at-a-time. Learning to read phonics is a step that is similar to crawling–reading stories right after learning the ABC's is like forcing children to run before they can crawl or walk. If dyslexic persons cannot spell, it means they were forced to run before they could crawl. Teachers need to undo that; they need to teach dyslexic persons phonics, wait for them to crawl and walk, and then running will take place naturally without force.

■ **Teach ESL Students Phonics even if they cannot Speak English:** From *Read Instantly*, ESL students who cannot yet speak English learn to read phonics in 1,400 basic but essential words; they do that similar to the way they learned to read the ABC's–we do not know the meaning of the ABC's, yet we learn to read them. ESL students do not have to know the meaning of a sound or a word in order to read it. After reading a word, they can look up its meaning.

■ **Introducing the First Spelling Pattern of a Long Vowel:** While the vast majority of sounds are still placed in a queue, one spelling pattern of each long vowel is then introduced. It is also justified logically by a spelling rule and then presented in a limited number of words. For instance, long "a" is first introduced as in "m**ai**n, r**ai**n, p**ai**n, t**ai**l, n**ai**l, etc." but not yet introduced as in d**ay**, **a**t**e**, **eigh**t, and t**a**bl**e**. Similarly, the long "e" is first introduced as in "m**ea**t" but not yet introduced as in m**ee**t, P**e**t**e**, **e**l**i**t**e**, rec**ei**ve, bel**ie**ve, m**e**, sk**i**, happ**y**, and monk**ey**.

■ **Simple Direct Instructions in *Read Instantly*:** Teachers are constantly reminded to avoid presenting a certain phonic that has not yet been introduced–they are asked to follow the same order of the lessons in the book. In fact, the phonics books by Camilia Sadik contain simple direct instructions and writing this *Teachers' Guide* is a result of pressure from traditional teachers who insist on having a separate guide.

■ **Everyone Learns to Read Instantly:** Learners are informed about a change that is about to occur before asking them to read any words that contain such change. For this reason, everyone learns to read from this book, without exceptions. Tutoring or teaching from *Read Instantly*, dyslexia in K-3 is easily prevented, and nonnative English speakers quickly learn to read phonics in words. Linguist Camilia Sadik spent over 15 years intensely dissecting English and preparing 10 phonics-based reading and spelling books for students to read and learn within days or weeks. Sadik insists that no one else needs to spend 15 years dissecting English in order to read or spell.

2. How to teach or learn from *Learn to Spell 500 Words a Day* by Camilia Sadik

Lean to Spell 500 Words a Day is a book in Six Volumes

Each volume is a 152-page colored textbook / workbook that contains over 2,200 words. The titles of the volumes are *The Vowel A*, *The Vowel E*, *The Vowel I*, *The Vowel O*, *The Vowel U*, and *The Consonants*. *The Vowel A* has five sounds spelled in 12 spelling patterns. *The Vowel E* has seven sounds spelled in 17 spelling patterns. *The Vowel I* has eight sounds spelled in 19 spelling patterns. *The Vowel O* has 12 sounds spelled in 20 spelling patterns. *The Vowel U* has six sounds spelled in 28 spelling patterns. Eight inconsistent *Consonants* have 50 sounds spelled in 60 spelling patterns.

■ **Comprehensive Book of Phonics for the Intermediate Level:** This is a comprehensive book of phonics; it contains nearly all the words of a specific sound and spelling pattern. For instance, the long ā sound spelled with the "**ai**" pattern as in "m**ai**n" occurs in approximately 210 English words. In *Read Instantly*, only 24 "ai" words are presented while in *Learn to Spell 500 Words a Day*, all 210 words are presented. In *Read Instantly*, each vowel is isolated in a chapter; but, in *Lean to Spell 500 Words a Day*, each vowel is isolated in a book. While *Read Instantly* is for beginners, this book is for the intermediate level and it teaches fluency in reading aloud and the spelling of 13,000 essential words.

■ **Spelling Rules in *Learn to Spell 500 Words a Day*:** Every one of the 360 phonics-based spelling lessons in *Learn to Spell 500 Words a Day* begins with logical explanations or a spelling rule. There are rules that govern the spelling phonics inside words and others that govern the spelling of phonics at the end of words. The spelling rules in *Learn to Spell 500 Words a Day* are mainly for inside words, and the spelling rules in *100 Spelling Rules* are mostly about word endings. Meanwhile, each rule is followed by nearly all the words that follow it and then by detailed practice lessons. *Learn to Spell 500 Words a Day* cannot be avoided; in it is the core and essence of the English language. Without it, *100 Spelling Rules* would not be easy for most learners. Most English speakers, who can read but cannot spell, can read this entire series of six volumes in six days.

■ **Sample Lessons from** *Learn to Spell 500 Words a Day*: *The Vowel A*: There are simple direct instructions before each lesson in all of the books. These six lessons about the long ā sound spelled with the "a-e" spelling pattern, as in "Jake" teach 414 words that can be learned in a 3-hour class.

Lesson 1: Meaning of a Long Vowel

The "a" is said to have a long sound when it sounds like the name of the letter **A**. The "a" as in "fate" sounds like the name of the letter **A**, and that makes it a long ā. Compare "fat" with "fate." The "a" in "fat" is a unique short sound of "a" that does not sound like the name of the letter **A**.

⊟Compare short ă with long ā in these words:

fat, fate	hat, hate	rat, rate	mat, mate
at, ate	fad, fade	tap, tape	plan, plane
pan, pane	pal, pale	mal, male	Al, ale
mad, made	Sam, same	dam, dame	

Lesson 2: The "a-e" Rule

We learned earlier in Chapter 1 that as in "rain," when two vowels "ai" are walking, the first one does the talking. This second rule in this chapter is built on the previous rule. According to this rule the two vowels can still walk together (help each other) in spite of having one consonant between them. Compare "fat" with "fate." As in "fate," one consonant between two vowels is too weak to keep the two vowels from helping each other (from walking together). This means that when there is only one consonant between two vowels, like the one "t" in "fate," that one "t" cannot keep the two vowels "a" and "e" away from each other (from walking together). The two vowels in "fate" can still help each other and walk together in this way "ā-e." The silent "e" can still help make the "a" long as if the two vowels were like this "ae" and as if the "t" were not between them. A dash as in "a-e" represents not only the "t" but any single consonant between two vowels, like the one "d" in "made." To prevent two vowels from walking, a consonant doubles before adding an "e" as in fat, fatter, fattest and this explains why consonants double.

fat or fate

Any single consonant between two vowels is too weak. As in "later," if the sound of "a" is long, we use one "t" after the "a." But, if the sound of "a" is short, we use "tt" after the "a" as in "latter." Likewise, we use one "p" after the long "a" as in "scraped" and "pp" after the short "a" as in "scrapped." This same rule applies to other vowels. For instance, we use one "n" after the long "i" in "diner" and "nn" after the short "i" in "dinner." We use one "p" after the long "o" in "hoped" and "pp" after the short "o" in "hopped." These are examples of any single consonant between two vowels being too weak: fate, theme, hope, dine, cure

Note: This "a-e" rule applies only to specific two vowels that fall in a syllable that is stressed. All such specific vowels are presented in this book. See these examples of any single consonant being weak between two vowels that fall in one stressed syllable: plane′, air·plane′; these′, Leb·a·nese′; side′, out·side′; scope′, mi′·cro·scope′; hope′, hope′·ful; fume′, per·fume′

Lesson 3: The "ā-*e*" phonic occurs in approximately 414 words

Read aloud to remember the spelling of these words, and read slowly to see the way words are spelled and to avoid seeing and writing letters in reverse. If in a classroom, students need to read aloud together in one rhythm. These are only 48 of the 414 words taken from *The Vowel A*:

Ja*ke*	ma*ke*	ca*ke*	sna*ke*
fa*ke*	ta*ke*	mis·ta*ke*	mis·tak·en
par·ta*ke*	sta*ke*	sa*ke*	for·sa*ke*
for·sak*en*	la*ke*	fla*ke*	snow·fla*ke*
flak*e*·y	flak*ed*	ra*ke*	rak*ed*
rak*es*	bra*ke*	wa*ke*	wak*es*
shak*es*	milk·sha*ke*	a·wa*ke*	a·wak·en
a·wak·en·ing	a·wak·en*ed*	qua*ke*	earth·qua*ke*
ba*ke*	bak*ed*	bak·ing	bak·er
bak·e·ry	ach*e*	ach*ed*	ach*es*
ach·y	back·ach*e*	stom·ach·ach*e*	tooth·ach*e*
ma*de*	re·ma*de*	gra*de*	up·gra*de*

Lesson 4: The "ā-*e*" words in a nonsensical story about "Ja*ke*"

Why Ja*ke*? Students remember the spelling of the "a-*e*" words by associating them with "Ja*ke*." Read aloud slowly whether you are in a classroom or alone:

Ja*ke* bak*es* his own ca*ke*. Ja*ke* eats ca*ke* when he wak*es*. Ja*ke* drinks milk·sha*ke* with his ca*ke*. Ja*ke* tak*es* his ca*ke* to the la*ke*. Ja*ke* lives clos*e* to a la*ke*. Ja*ke* wak*es* to ta*ke* a wa*l*k. Etc. The rest of this story is on a few pages in *The Vowel A*.

38

Lesson 5: Do we spell with "**a**-**e**" (mad**e**) or with "**ai**" (m**ai**d)?

⊟Compare the "**a**-**e**" and the "**ai**" patterns in these words that sound the same (homonyms):

mad*e*, m**ai**d	bat*e*, b**ai**t	plan*e*, pl**ai**n	pan*e*, p**ai**n
pal*e*, p**ai**l	mal*e*, m**ai**l	sal*e*, s**ai**l	tal*e*, t**ai**l
star*e*, st**ai**r	far*e*, f**ai**r	par*e*, p**ai**r	wast*e*, w**ai**st
wav*e*, w**ai**v*e*			

Consider this theory for spelling with "a-*e*" or "ai"

▪ First, verbs are more important than nouns, and nouns are more important than adjectives.

▪ Second, the people who developed written English liked the "**a**-**e**" more than "**ai**."

▪ Therefore, in words that sounded the same, they seemed to favor using "**a**-**e**" in verbs as in "mad*e*" and "**ai**" in nouns as in "m**ai**d." Moreover, in words that sounded the same, they favored using "**a**-**e**" in nouns as in "plan*e*" and "**ai**" in adjectives as in "pl**ai**n." Furthermore, if any of these words can be both a verb and a noun too, it most likely is spelled with an "**ai**." For example, "m**ai**l" can be both a verb and a noun, and it is spelled with an "**ai**."

Lesson 6: Compare "a-*e*" with "ai"

Try to remember some of these words as they were used in the previous stories about "El**ai**n*e*" and "Jak*e*." For instance, "Jak*e*" was the one who had an "airplan*e*" and "El**ai**n*e*" was the one who ate "pl**ai**n" yogurt. The "**ai**" and "**a**-**e**" words were separated for you in two different stories. You may go back and read the two stories aloud as many times as needed, until you are can remember the words being used in the stories.

⊟Compare the "**a**-**e**" as in "Jak*e*" with the "**ai**" as in "El**ai**n*e*":

• El**ai**n*e* is the one who at*e* **plain** yo·gurt.

• Jak*e* is the one who had an air·**plane** and it was an old **plane**.

• El**ai**n*e* was the one who had a **maid**, and Jak*e* **made** a cak*e*.

• El**ai**n*e*'s **mail** was de·lay*e*d. Jak*e* had one **male** friend.

• El**ai**n*e*'s **pail** was fill*e*d with rain and hail. Jan*e* look*e*d **pale**.

• El**ai**n*e* had a **sail**·bo*a*t. Jak*e*'s plan*e* was for **sale**.

• El**ai**n*e* had a pony·**tail**. Jak*e* didn't finish tell·ing his **tale**.

• El**ai**n*e*'s wa·ter fees were **waived** af·ter the rain.

• Jak*e* couldn't see him·self **waving** good·by*e* to Dav*e*.

• Jak*e* stepp*e*d on his car's **brakes** be·for*e* he ran o·ver a **snake**.

39

3. How to teach or learn from *100 Spelling Rules* by Camilia Sadik

100 Spelling Rules is for the Advanced Level

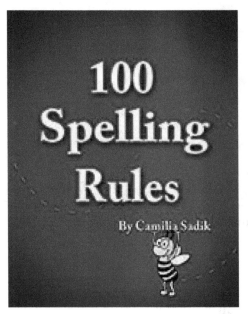

Linguist Camilia Sadik discovered more than 100 spelling rules. This 250-page colored textbook and workbook is for the advanced level. If students are advanced, they can learn from this book with or without the help of a teacher. If they are not advanced, they need to learn from the preceding books to become advances and then return to this book. *100 Spelling Rules* teaches the spelling of 12,000 multi-syllabic words. Most of the rules in *100 Spelling Rules* are about spelling suffixes and word endings.

Simple Direct Instructions

100 Spelling Rules contains 105 spelling lessons. Each lesson begins with a question, the question is followed by a spelling rule or many spelling rules, and then nearly all the words that follow a rule are listed. In the end, students are asked to read the words aloud to memorize the spelling of hundreds of words at-a-time.

Two Sample Lessons taken from *100 Spelling Rules*

Lesson 1: Do we spell with "cial" as in "social" or with "tial" as in "essential"?

Rule Spell with "cial" after a vowel as in "social" and with "tial" after a consonant as in "essential."

Details The "cial" and "tial" endings occur in approximately **38** words.

Practice

vowel + cial in 11 words

fa·cial	ra·cial	gla·cial	of·fi·cial
ben·e·fi·cial	ar·ti·fi·cial	su·per·fi·cial	ju·di·cial
spe·cial	cru·cial	so·cial	

consonant + tial in 20 words

res·i·den·tial	pres·i·den·tial	cre·den·tial	pru·den·tial

40

con·fi·den·**tial**   po·ten·**tial**   ex·is·ten·**tial**   in·flu·en·**tial**

ref·er·en·**tial**   es·sen·**tial**   se·quen·**tial**   con·se·quen·**tial**

sub·stan·**tial**   cir·cum·stan·**tial**   ex·pe·ri·en·**tial**   par·**tial**

mar·**tial**   nup·**tial**   pre·nup·**tial**   tan·gen·**tial**

Exceptions: Memorize these seven exceptions–the word "controver**s**ial" contradicts all the rules because it is spelled with an "**s**."

fi·nan·**cial**   com·mer·**cial**   pro·vin·**cial**   in·i·**tial**

spa·**tial**   pa·la·**tial**   con·tro·ver·**sial**

Read the above 38 words aloud as many times as needed until you memorize their spelling.

Copy the above 38 words and do not try to guess their spelling. Look at each word before you begin to copy it and do not look away from it until you are 100% confident that you can spell it:

Fill in the blanks using the endings "cial" or "tial" or "sial":

so _ _ _ _   essen _ _ _ _   spe _ _ _ _

fa _ _ _ _   offi _ _ _ _   substan _ _ _ _

creden _ _ _ _   residen _ _ _ _   artifi _ _ _ _

consequen _ _ _ _   ra _ _ _ _   poten _ _ _ _

confiden _ _ _ _   circumstan _ _ _ _   cru _ _ _ _

pruden _ _ _ _   gla _ _ _ _   referen _ _ _ _

benefi _ _ _ _   influen _ _ _ _   judi _ _ _ _

nup _ _ _ _   par _ _ _ _   mar _ _ _ _

prenup _ _ _ _   spa _ _ _ _   pala _ _ _ _

ini _ _ _ _   finan _ _ _ _   commer _ _ _ _ provin _ _ _ _   contraver _ _ _ _   so _ _ _ _ ly

essen _ _ _ _ ly   spe _ _ _ _ ly   offi _ _ _ _ ly

par _ _ _ _ ly   ini _ _ _ _ ly   finan _ _ _ _ ly

commer _ _ _ _ ly   commer _ _ _ _ ized   existen _ _ _ _

existen _ _ _ _ ism   existen _ _ _ _ ist   cru _ _ _ _ ly

congen _ _ _ _

Lesson 2: Do we spell with "**f**" as in "font," "**ph**" as in "geogra**ph**y," or "**gh**" as in "enou**gh**"?

Rule The letter "**f**" is not allowed long words, and if a word is long (more than one or two syllables) as in "geogra**ph**y," then the sound of "**f**" is spelled with a "**ph**." Note that the origin of the "**ph**" is derived from the Greek language. As in "enou**gh**," the "**gh**" that sounds like an "**f**" occurs in approximately **seven** words.

Practice

gh occurs in 7 words

e·nou**gh**	tou**gh**	rou**gh**
cou**gh**	lau**gh**	slou**gh**
trou**gh**	sou**gh**	

The following **39** words are examples of a countless number of long words that contain a "**ph**." Remember that the "**f**" is not allowed in long words:

ge·og·ra·**ph**y	**ph**i·los·o·**ph**y	bi·og·ra·**ph**y
au·to·bi·og·ra·**ph**y	a·pos·tro·**ph**e	pe·ri**ph**·er·al
hy·**ph**en·at·ed	ne**ph**·ew	at·mos·**ph**er*e*
eu·**ph**e·mism	**ph**y·si·cian	**Ph**i·la·del·**ph**i·a
Phi·lip·pin*e*	am·**ph**ib·i·an	am·**ph**i·the·a·ter
so·**ph**is·ti·cat·ed	gra**ph**·ics	el·e·**ph**ant
phar·ma·cy	**ph**ar·ma·cist	al·**ph**a·bet

em·**pha**·siz*e*	em·**pha**·sis	sym·**pho**·ny
pho·nol·o·gy	**pho**·bic	**phon**·ics
pho·net·ic	**pho**·nem*e*	met·a·**phor**
pho·to·gra**ph**	tri·um**ph**	par·a·gra**ph**
pam·**ph**let	o**ph**·thal·mol·o·gy	di**ph**·thong
schiz·o·**phre**·ni·a	par·a·**phras**e	*Eu*·**phra**·tes

🐦 **Exceptions**: The following **21** words are exceptions because they are relatively long, yet spelled with an "f," not with a "ph." Either memorize these words or know that the stem "fer" is Latin, not Greek and we do not use a "ph" in Latin words. In addition, the "f" in these words may be followed by a consonant as in "**fl**uency," while the "ph" is normally followed by a vowel except in the three words **phr**ase, schizo**phr**enia, and Eu**phr**ates. Note that in this book a long word means a word that has more than one or two syllables.

f occurs in 21 relatively long words:

re·fer	pre·fer	trans·fer
fel·o·ny	fem·i·nin*e*	fi·nit*e*
fi·del·i·ty	in·fant	fa·nat·ic
fab·u·lous	fa·cil·i·tat*e*	fam·i·ly
fan·ta·sy	fal·la·cy	fan·tas·tic
fam·in*e*	com·fort	fu·gi·tiv*e*
fu·ri·ous	fur·ni·ture	ref·ug*e*

☝ Read all the above words aloud as many times as needed until you memorize their spelling.

✎ Make a copy of page 16, which is a lined page, and then copy all the above words in lesson 2. Know that anytime you are asked to copy words, do not try to guess their spelling. Instead, look at each word before you begin to copy it and do not look away from it until you are 100% confident that you can spell it.

✎ Fill in the blanks using f, ff, ph, or gh:

photogra _ _   sym _ _ ony   sa _ e

cou _ _   _ _ armacist   geogra _ _ y

43

enou _ _

Christo _ _ er

_ _ iloso _ _ y

meta _ _ or

tou _ _

so _ _ isticated

am _ _ ibian

com _ _ ort

schizo _ _ renia

Ste _ _ anie

_ ont

re _ _ erence

_ urniture

cou _ _ ing

stu _ _

_ ree

al _ _ abet

lau _ _

paragra _ _

_ ew

Je _ _

trans _ er

rou _ _

para _ _ rase

rou _ _

pre _ _ er

pre _ _ erence

_ antastic

lau _ _ ing

stu _ _ ed

_ _ ysician

ele _ _ ant

_ _ onics

autobiogra _ _ y

ne _ _ ew

am _ _ itheater

_ _ ase

mu _ _ ler

di _ _ icult

hy _ _ en

pre _ _ erred

_ ur

_ abulous

rou _ _ ly

stu _ _ ing

4. How to teach or learn from *The Compound Words* by Camilia Sadik

The Compound Words is for Children and Adults

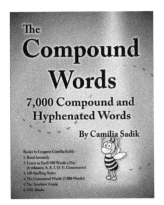

The Compound Words is a workbook for learning over **5,000** compound words and **2,000** hyphenated words. The 7,000 words in this book are grouped alphabetically, colored, and prepared for children and adults to simply read and learn their spelling. For instance, 106 compound words and 29 hyphenated words that begin with an "a" are listed on three pages.

With the help of a teacher, *The Compound Words* can be for children of any age. It is also for older children and adults who can read but cannot spell the words that they read.

Teachers or parents may use their judgment for when and what age to use this book or parts of this book. If your student can read and spell the two words "home" and "work," then it is appropriate to teach him or her the word "homework."

After learning to spell the parts that a compound word is made of, learning to spell a compound word can be achieved by simply looking at it.

If one wishes to memorize the spelling of hundreds of words at-a-time, one will need to read the 7,000 words aloud as many times as needed until they are all memorized.

Sample Lessons from the Compound Words

A

after

afterbirth	aftercare	afterlife
afterworld	afterimage	aftereffect
aftermath	aftershock	aftertaste
afterglow	afterpiece	afterthought
aftershave	aftertime	afternoon
aftermarket	aftermost	afterdamp
afterdeck	afterburner	afterward
afterwards		

air

airmail	airplane	airport
airline	airmobile	aircraft
antiaircraft	airship	airfare
airborne	airbrush	airburst
airfield	airflow	airfoil
airframe	airbag	airbrake
airbladder	airframe	airfreight
airglow	airhead	airplay
airsickness	airless	airspace
airstrip	airtight	airwave
airworthy		

any

anybody	anyone	anyhow
anyway	anyways	anymore
anyplace	anything	anytime
anywhere	anywise	

arm

| armpit | armhole | armlet |
| armrest | | |

arch

archbishop	archdeacon	archdiocese
archduke	archducal	archduchess
archduchy	archway	archerfish

aweless	awestruck	awesome
anglesite	angleworm	
alongshore	alongside	
alderwomen	alderman	
alewife	alehouse	
almshouse	almsman	
allover	allspice	
applesauce	applejack	
assemblyman	assemblywoman	
artwork	artless	
arrowhead	arrowroot	
artilleryman	angelfish	alleyway
areaway	aromatherapy	authorship
addlebrained		

A-

all-

all-day	all-embracing	all-friend
all-important	all-inclusive	all-or-nothing
all-out	all-powerful	all-purpose
all-around	all-star	all-time
all-terrain	all-right	alright, all right
air-to-air	air-traffic control	
apple-pie	apple-polish	

across-the-board   aide-de-camp   airy-fairy

almond-eyed   around-the-clock   attorney-at-law

accented-lantern

⬆ Practice of all the above words: Read the above words aloud slowly as many times as needed until you memorize their spelling.

✍ Copy the above compound & hyphenated words that begin with an **A**. Look at each word before you begin to copy it; do not try to guess its spelling:

_____   _____   _____   _____

_____   _____   _____   _____

_____   _____   _____   _____

_____   _____   _____   _____

_____   _____   _____   _____

_____   _____   _____   _____

_____   _____   _____   _____

_____   _____   _____   _____

5. How to teach Spoken English and Reading Phonics to ESL Students

Teach Spoken English Using Sentence Pattern

Teach spoken English in sentence patters, not in fixed sentences that require memorizing one fixed sentence at-a-time. Speed and fluency in spoken English is better achieved when students use the same sentence pattern and repeat it out loud in 10 sentences. For instance, the sentence pattern is "I have a book." and students are asked to replace the word "book." with any singular noun that they may know and say that in 10 sentences.

The goal is to achieve fluency in saying 10 sentences using the same "I have a book." pattern. Also, students need to keep repeating the 10 sentences until they achieve fluency in this pattern. Only after achieving speed and fluency in one pattern, are students allowed to learn a new pattern. Each learned pattern will be stored in their brain like a brick is in building a house.

The author class-tested the 10 sentences per pattern method and students spoke from the first day of class. Because students were more than willing to speak, the author divided students into groups, wherein one speaks and one listens and supports the other with no interruptions or corrections. When teachers became overwhelmed with the number of students who wanted to speak, they asked students to record their speech on tape.

■ **Teach Reading Phonics to ESL Students even if They cannot Speak English:** From *Read Instantly*, ESL students who cannot yet speak English learn to read phonics in 1,400 basic but essential words; they do that similar to the way they learned to read the ABC's–we do not know the meaning of the ABC's, yet we learn to read them. ESL students do not have to know the meaning of a sound or a word in order to read it. After reading a word, they can look up its meaning.

Together the two textbooks *Read Instantly* and *English for Nonnative English Speakers* are ideal for teaching phonics and spoken English as a second language in schools around the globe.

Sample Lessons taken from *English for Nonnative English Speakers*

The Home: Students learn the vocabulary, the accurate pronunciation, and the use of nearly all the items that exist in a typical American home–they learn the meaning of over 400 household items, one room at-a-time.

After learning the meaning and pronunciation of each word, students read aloud the same words isolated and then in a specific sentence pattern. Following that, they are asked to close the book and say 10 sentences per each pattern. They repeat until they are completely fluent in that pattern. Being fluent in 10 sentences of the same pattern is like building a brick in a home.

Read aloud slowly:

✓ a hous*e*, a door, a ki*t*ch·en, a bed·room, a bath·room, a liv·ing room, etc.
I see a hous*e*. I see a door. I see a ki*t*ch·en. I see a bed·room. I see a bath·room. I see a liv·ing room. Etc. Note that students must achieve fluency in 10 sentences using the "I see" sentence pattern before moving to next pattern–they ought to follow several rules in this method, which are stated in the book.

✓ an **a**·part·ment, an **ad**·dress, an **at**·tic, an **ap**·ple, an **e**gg, an **ov**·en, etc.
I need an **a**·part·ment. I need an **ad**·dress. I need an **at**·tic. I need an **ap**·ple. I need an **e**gg. I need an **ov**·en. Etc.

✓ door, room, book, bed·room, pen, pin, pill, hat, etc.
This is a door. This is a room. This is a book. This is a bed·room. This is a pen. This is a pin. This is a pill. This is a hat. Etc.

✓ doors, rooms, stairs, books, bed·rooms, pens, pins, pills, hats, etc.
These are doors. These are rooms. These are stairs. These are books. These are bed·rooms. These are pens. These are pins. These are pills. These are hats. Etc.

✓ doors, rooms, books, bed·rooms, pens, pins, pills, hats, etc.
I have doors. I have rooms. I have books. I have bed·rooms. I have pens. I have pins. I have pills. I have hats. Etc.

✓ Students read the above sentences aloud slowly as many times as need and then close their books and say the "This is a book." pattern in any 10 sentences until they achieve speed and fluency in it. They may record 10 sentences for each pattern they learned on tape and then give the tape to their teacher or tutor for evaluations and feedback:
This is a hous*e*. This is a liv·ing room. This is a din·ing room. This is a bed·room. This is a bath·room. This is a ki*t*ch·en. This is a clock. This is a book. This is a fan. Etc.

Note: Linguist Camilia Sadik has been working hard to produce various ESL books.

Simple Direct Instruction before Each Lesson

Every lesson begins with easy-to-follow direct instructions for teachers to read and then explain to students. Teachers may read each comment before a new practice lesson and explain it to students. For instances, teachers may read about the meaning of a concept like "schwa" and then explain that to students. They may read about the importance of "students reading aloud slowly" and then explain that. They may read a specific "spelling rule" and explain it–students will then read aloud the practice lesson that follows that rule.

Usually, students, who finish learning from *Read Instantly*, are capable of reading and comprehending these instructions, they can learn to spell without the help of a teacher. In fact, this *Teachers' Guide* is not necessary because most of what is in it is available in the books. Lessons are explicit and self-explanatory. The actual reason for having this guide is to satisfy traditional teachers who insist on having a teacher's edition.

The following teaching instructions are a few of many taken from the books:

1 Direct instruction before every lesson: There are simple direct instructions at the beginning of each new lesson for teachers to read and then explain to students.

2 Grouping of words of a similar sound and spelling pattern is prepared for you in each lesson; simply teach the same words and the nonsensical stories that follow the lists of words.

3 Pay attentions to students with a logical learning style: English was written for memorizers, but logical learners cannot memorize without logical explanations as to why a sound should be spelled one-way and not the other. They are so logical; they expect to see "electrician" to be "electrision" or "electrition." Students with a logical learning style are the majority in your class but are not always capable of diagnosing the reason for knowing how to spell.

4 Disallow speed-reading before learning to spell: Forced speed-reading before learning to spell causes students to see letters in reverse, and then spelling them in reverse. Dyslexia in spelling and in writing letters in reverse ends, after learning to spell and after slowing down to write words slowly.

5 Vowels rule English and they cannot be avoided: Explain that to students and ask them to focus their vision on the vowels when they read. Inform them that learning the 38 sounds and 96 spelling patterns of vowel is the most important part of learning to read and spell.

6 Do not force learning and do not stop too long to memorize the spelling of every single word. Learning to spell is acquired naturally as students keep reading aloud slowly.

7 Explain gradually the symbols and concepts used in the books and as needed. For instance, explain that *Italic letters* represent silent letters, like the silent *p* in recei*p*t.

8 Insist on students reading aloud: Students must be informed from the first day of class that the way we acquire information is through our five senses, and teachers need to show them how that works. Continue to insist until they read all the practice lessons aloud, whether in or outside of the classroom. If in a classroom, they need to read aloud together in one rhythm.

A convincing example: Narrate this convincing example about an imaginary ten-year old child who was born with a perfect brain, but without any of his five senses. Suppose that someone in the same room with that child poured hot coffee in a cup. How will that child learn what coffee is if he cannot **see** it or **hear** it pour or **feel** its heat or **taste** it or **smell** it? Naturally, that child would not learn what coffee means. By giving this example from the first day of class, you will convince students that we acquire information through our senses.

> **All the practice lessons must be read aloud by students.**
>
> **If in a classroom, students need to read aloud together in one rhythm.**

The next step is to apply the child's example to learning to read and spell by using three of one's senses simultaneously. Students need to know that when reading aloud, they are seeing the word, hearing it, and feeling it in their mouths as they utter it. Not only does using the three senses together make learning possible, but it also speeds up the memorization process. It is through the senses that any piece of information is registered into the memory portion of the brain. Without reading the practice lessons aloud, students will understand a rule but will not remember to spell the words that follow that rule. When the entire class is reading aloud, students hear more sounds and thus remember more. Students' reading aloud is critical for this method to work.

9 The Understanding before Memorization Approach (UBMA): The vast majority of older children and up and adults need to understand a subject before they can memorize it. After applying more than 100 easy rules that govern phonics and English spelling, students understand when to spell a sound one-way and not the other.

10 The Students Reading Aloud Slowly Approach (S-RASA): Unless followed by immediate practice lessons, understanding alone does not lead to remembering the spelling of words. The Students Reading Aloud Slowly Approach is for memorizing the spelling of words. S-RASA differs from the parents or teachers reading aloud to students. Instead, it is about the students, themselves, reading aloud and using three of their senses simultaneously. Learners need not force memorization; they learn to spell naturally through applying the UBMA and the **S-RASA**. Both approaches were developed and class-tested by Linguist Camilia Sadik.

11 Why reading slowly? In the beginning, reading slowly allows new learners to take the time needed to see how words are spelled. The ultimate goal is to prepare students to read for comprehension. Allow students the time needed to see what follows a vowel in order to read it and spell it correctly. For instance, they need time to see what follows the vowel "i" in "niece" to avoid seeing it as "nice." The structure of English is that reading a vowel requires seeing what follows that vowel before reading it. If any student is reading too fast for the rest of his or her classmates, stop them and ask them to be considerate and read slowly.

12 **Do not force speed-reading:** When students are forced to move their visions too quickly, from left-to-right and from right-to-left, they end up seeing letters in reverse and then spelling letters in reverse. Spelling letters in reverse is dyslexia. Specifically, do not force logical learners into speed-reading; logical learners are slower because they think and analyze before they can memorize. Besides, speed-reading is acquired naturally after each learner is allowed enough time to acquire it in his or her own pace.

13 **Understanding is not enough without practice lessons:** Without immediately reading the practice lessons aloud, students may understand a spelling rule but will not memorize the actual spelling of words, and there is a difference between understanding a rule and memorizing the words that follow that rule. Therefore, it is best for students to continue to read aloud all the practice lessons in this entire program before they are asked to write anything. Up to 50 students may read aloud together in one classroom. If any student (s) is unable to keep up with the class' pace or rhythm, teachers need to ask half of the class to read first while the other half listens, and then rotate. If one is not in a classroom, one may read aloud alone.

14 **Spelling a word without guessing:** Avoid guessing the spelling of a word. Instead, look at a word before you spell it. Only after achieving confidence that you can spell a word, should you look away from it to spell it.

15 **Students need to take all the time needed to spell a word**: Beginners need to take a moment to think which spelling pattern of a sound to choose when spelling a word. They need to know that they are not alone in needing time to spell–everyone must think about that because this is the way English is. If writing in too big of a hurry, even good spellers can make mistakes like this, "I here you speak and I eat meet" and spell checkers do not catch such slips either. Students need to take all the time needed to spell a word–they need not hurry to impress anyone who may be watching them spell. Speed in spelling will be acquired naturally, not through force. In fact, achieving speed in anything is acquired naturally, not through force.

16 **Simple Equation:** Students need to relax, understand the logic behind spelling, not force memorization, and read the practice lessons aloud slowly. They need not be too concerned with remembering the spelling of every word, because learning takes place naturally and without them realizing it. They may apply the simple equation of relaxing + understanding the logic + reading aloud slowly + repetition → memory.

17 **What is dyslexia in spelling?** Dyslexia in spelling is an acquired condition whereby logical learners can have difficulties when reading or spelling words, plus they spell letters in reverse. Usually, dyslexic persons were forced to speed-read before learning to spell words. They were forced to quickly shift their vision from left-to- right and from right-to-left. In their haste, they saw letters in reverse, and then they spelled them in that same reversed manner that they saw them and read them. Note that being a logical learner is hereditary but not being dyslexic.

18 **Why can't we spell?** The reason we can't spell is that one English sound can be spelled in a number of ways called spelling patterns. Most of us can read the numerous spelling patterns of a sound but do not always remember which of the numerous patterns to choose when spelling that sound in words. For instance, we may read "musician" but spell it "musision" or "musition."

19 **Inform students with spelling difficulties that they are not alone**: According to reliable sources, half of the adults in the U.S. are not able to read books written at an eighth-grade level. The U.S. News and World Report says, "It is forecasted that the decline in reading skills will lead in two decades to an elite, literate class of no more than 30% of the population."

20 **Raise Students' Self-esteem:** From the first day of class, teachers need to inform students who have reading or spelling difficulties that the problem is not in them, but in the fact that one English sound is spelled in many different ways. Immediately, they need to stop blaming themselves for not being able to remember the correct spelling of words.

Before the discovery of over 100 spelling rules, learning phonics was based strictly on memorization. Too many people who had reading or spelling difficulties were led to believe that they had learning disabilities. People had to memorize, without logic, which spelling pattern of a phonic to choose when spelling a sound in every English word.

21 **Logical learners cannot focus on more than one thing at a time:** They cannot focus on the way words are spelled while reading for comprehension. In fact, they cannot focus on any two things at a time. Traditional educators are unaware of this fact; thus, they continue to ask students to read more stories, hoping that in the process students will learn to spell. Only memorizers do not require regularity or logic. Logical learners are the better thinkers because they question things that do not make sense. The fact of the matter is that most people with spelling difficulties are more creative because they can focus highly on one thing and then become creative in that one thing. Albert Einstein could not spell and he is a fine example of such highly focused and creative persons.

22 **Characteristics shared by dyslexic persons:** Dyslexic persons can learn and are not learning disabled; they learn to spell when logic is provided. They are not visual and cannot visualize faces or the way words are spelled. They can only focus on one thing or one thought at a time. They are perfectionists needing a long time to finish their work; all work to them must be creative or they may not finish it. They tend to be unhappy when disturbed while doing their creative work. Most dyslexic persons misspell words, write letters in reverse, stumble when reading aloud, have difficulties spelling words orally, miss their exists if driving and someone is talking with them, have car accidents when text messaging and driving, some write all of the letters in uppercase, and most are wrongly led to believe that they have learning disabilities.

Comprehensive pre- and post-spelling tests by Camilia Sadik, © 1998

Note to Teachers:

Please try to administer these spelling tests before and after teaching from all of the books by Camilia Sadik. These tests are to measure the effectiveness of this program. Students will use the same tests before and after learning. These tests are comprehensive because every phonic is represented in, at least, a word or two. Give one point for each word, and the total points are 260 points:

Test #1

1. maintain	2. available	3. explain	4. entertain
5. plain yogurt	6. paid	7. curtain	8. fatter
9. snack	10. snake	11. made	12. airplane
13. vase	14. neighbor	15. sausage	16. faucet
17. author	18. audience	19. awkward	20. awesome
21. dawn	22. thaw	23. false	24. hallway
25. bake	26. backward	27. daughter	28. beggar
29. caution	30. acquaintances	31. played	32. praying
33. latter	34. later	35. stopping	36. stomachache
37. exhausted	38. restaurant	39. sweet	40. redeem
41. self-esteem	42. succeed	43. precede	44. feast
45. wheat	46. yeast	47. impeach	48. cheat
49. complete	50. elite	51. petite	52. sincere
53. chief	54. extreme	55. Japanese	56. chef
57. piece	58. believe	59. niece	60. raspberry
61. receipt	62. protein	63. donkey	64. lucky
65. valley	66. attorney	67. team	68. chemistry
69. letter	70. litter	71. bikini	72. reddest
73. stepped	74. reddest	75. ski	76. spelling
77. sweater	78. sign	79. juice	80. hide
81. tie	82. light	83. trying	84. pry
85. pray	86. cot	87. coat	88. joke
89. boil	90. bitter	91. require	92. cute
93. cutter	94. fruit	95. super	96. supper
97. continue	98. Europe	99. nephew	**100**. curfew

Test # 2

1. activities	2. steady	3. wealthier	4. happiness
5. pleasant	6. already	7. ballot	8. gourmet
9. marriage	10. difficulties	11. luckily	12. carried
13. insight	14. trying	15. hid	16. analyze
17. thigh	18. tried	19. hide	20. typing
21. sign	22. tries	23. file	24. hydraulics
25. design	26. signifies	27. define	28. dynasty
29. rewind	30. sacrifice	31. bitter	32. spiral
33. tie	34. bite	35. bicycle	36. guy
37. surprise	38. bypass	39. pry	40. pray
41. liar	42. compromise	43. riddle	44. ally
45. alley	46. good-bye	47. generalize	48. fill
49. reply	50. lying	51. memorize	52. guilt
53. difference	54. committed	55. diner	56. cries
57. slipped	58. onion	59. thinner	60. dinner
61. cried	62. coach	63. facial	64. vowel
65. choir	66. require	67. hopped	68. consonant
69. jogging	70. syllable	71. touch	72. soldier
73. forty	74. double	75. foes	76. taught
77. of course	78. postage	79. noun	80. caught
81. hoped	82. employ	83. boots	84. bought
85. cutter	86 cuter	87. supper	88. super
89. sue	90. argue	91. continue	92. suitcase
93. juice	94. tube	95. Europe	96. neurotic
97. nephew	98. Hebrew	99. curfew	100. menu

Test # 3

1. enclosed	2. boil	3. choose	4. fought
5. boredom	6. noise	7. chose	8. governor
9. slowly	10. joints	11. donor	12. professor
13. controversial	14. musician	15. evidence	16. educator
17. usually	18. continuous	19. humorous	20. review
21. tomb	22. coup	23. virus	24. various
25. millennium	26. delicious	27. obnoxious	28. anxious
29. fictitious	30. structure	31. equal	32. liquid
33. extinguisher	34. guess	35. ghost	36. guide
37. tough	38. mission	39. technician	40. expression
41. business	42. busy	43. build	44. cousin
45. college	46. package	47. chemistry	48. excel
49. until	50.secretary	51. attendance	52. realize
53. surprise	54. television	55. separate	56. historical
57. article	58. substantial	59. dessert	60. principal

8

Why can't we spell?

The reason we can't spell is that a single English sound can be spelled in many different ways. Most of us can read the numerous spelling patterns of the various English sounds; but, we do not always remember which of the numerous patterns to choose when spelling these sounds in words. For instance, we may read ocean, but spell it ocian, osion, oshion, otion, oceon, etc.

The long ē sound alone is spelled in **10** spelling patterns, as in me, meet, meat, receive, believe, happy, money, ski, complete, and elite. The "k" sound is spelled in five spelling patterns, as in keep, cloud, chemistry, maximum, and queen. Imagine having to memorize, without any logical structure, the spelling of over 180 spelling patterns of more than 90 sounds in a countless number of words! The latter examples were only a few of many to show why we can't spell in English.

Two Types of Learners with Two Types of Learning Styles

There are two types of learners that I named memorizers and analyzers. Memorizers have a visual learning style and analyzers have a logical learning style.

Memorizers are born with a visual learning style; they can simply look at a word and memorize its spelling. Without logic, they simply visualize a word and remember it as if they were taking a picture of it.

Analyzers are born with a logical learning style and they cannot memorize anything that does not make sense to them. They cannot look at a word and memorize its spelling; instead, they require logical explanations or spelling rules to show them when to spell a sound one-way and not the other. It makes no sense to them to spell "nose" with an "s" unless they are informed beforehand that the "s" can sound like a "z" when between two vowels.

Being an Analyzer is Hereditary but not being a Poor Speller

Reliable researchers have produced a correlation between functional and structural differences in the brains of children. They confirmed that the brain wiring of a poor speller differs from that of a person who is a good speller.

Based on brain differences, traditional researchers concluded that poor spellers have neurological learning deficiencies, which are innate in nature. Their argument may look valid because such persons do have spelling or reading difficulties, but the argument is unsound because it is based on false premises.

There is a huge difference between having a "different wiring" and "brain deficiencies." Naturally, the wiring of a logical learner's brain differs from that which is less analytic. However, this does entail a deficiency in anyone's brain. One might argue that memorizers have brain deficiencies, because their brains are wired differently and because they memorize without questioning the logic behind what they are about to memorize. Furthermore, one might argue that poor spellers are the better thinkers because they examine what they are about to memorize, or that they are the finest type of learners because they require logic first, or that they are the most creative ones because of the great number of creative persons who are poor spellers.

Persons with spelling difficulties do NOT have neurological learning deficiencies; perhaps those who don't understand them do. Naturally, a brain of a very logical person will be wired differently from that of a memorizer who does not question or analyze as much. However, this does not entail a deficiency in anyone's brain. There is a difference between having a different wiring system in the brain and having a brain deficiency. One can claim that memorizers have brain deficiencies, because their brains are wired differently and because they memorize without questioning the logic behind what they are about to memorize.

When the same researchers learn more about logical learners and the illogical way English words are spelled, they will be convinced that being a logical learner is hereditary but being a poor speller is not hereditary.

Typically, memorizers think everyone learns as they do, and they have no clue how analyzers learn. Some memorizers say, "Why do you need logic or spelling rules? Just look at words and learn to spell them." Obviously, English was written for memorizers, not for analyzers. Because they can spell, memorizers often occupy authoritative positions, deciding how the rest of us should be taught and how our brains are deformed or not deformed.

Only Analytic Learners can have Spelling Difficulties in English

If no logic or spelling rules are provided, analyzers are the ones who can have spelling difficulties. In fact, logical learners are always searching for reasons that make sense to help them memorize the spelling of English words. So far, we have established that lack of logic causes analyzers to have spelling difficulties in English.

Not All Languages have Poor Spelling

Most known languages have a consistent same letter or same symbol to represent a single sound, every time that sound is written in words. Such languages might use the letter "f" in font, symphony, enough, and in all the words that contain an "f" sound. In such languages students do not have to memorize which spelling pattern of the "f" sound to choose. Hence, spelling difficulties are eliminated and so are remedial reading programs or special education departments in schools or community colleges.

Italian, Spanish, Japanese, Chinese, and Arabic are a few such languages. In fact, most new immigrants, who are completely literate in their native tongues, come to the U.S. and then have spelling difficulties in English. Moreover, they send their children to schools assuming that they will learn to read and spell in the same way that they learned when they were in their homelands. Most had not heard of a child going to school, passing from one grade to another without learning to read or spell. Children with reading and spelling problems in one language might not have one in a different language. If logical English speakers were born into a language that has one spelling pattern (one symbol) per sound, they would not be poor spellers in that language.

Poor Spelling begins before the 4th Grade

Logical children can only memorize after seeing the logic behind what they are about to memorize. Logical children are the ones who can become poor spellers or they may not read at all. Children with reading and /or spelling difficulties are usually diagnosed as such in the 4th grade. When phonics is taught randomly in bits and pieces and without logical spelling rules, logical kids will become poor spellers before the 4th grade.

High Illiteracy Rate among English Speakers

According to reliable statistics, most of us have a severe or a mild case of illiteracy in English. Some of us can read and comprehend, but cannot always spell the words that we read; others cannot read at all, or read below their grade level. Typically, logical learners can get by and pass in schools because their teachers can understand what the words mean when spelled like this, "We uzed to meat hear every weak."

Several Types of Dyslexia

Dyslexia in **speech** is, as in saying aks for ask.

Dyslexia in **spelling** letters in reverse is, as in spelling shipment as shipmetn.

Dyslexia in **reading** words in reverse is, as in reading my nice is niece.

Dyslexia in **writing** words in reverse is, as in writing tree birds on three.

When people are intimidated, pressured or forced to hurry, they may do anything in reverse. Interestingly, each thing people can do in reverse has a name nowadays; writing numbers in reverse is called dyscalculia.

Classic Definitions of Dyslexia

Dyslexia has no single definition; there are over 70 definitions of dyslexia. However, classic signs of dyslexia are associated with language difficulties, as in reading and / or spelling difficulties or both, and letter reversal. Some see dyslexia as learning disability, neurological deficiency, or poor or inadequate vision or hearing.

Usually, when no one knows why a child has reading or spelling difficulties, the easiest and most accessible label placed on that child is "dyslexia" and the easiest and most irresponsible explanation of what dyslexia might mean is "learning disability" or "neurological learning disorder." Reality is that there is too much unnecessary commotion created around dyslexia when the spotlight should have been on "the illogical way words are spelled."

What is dyslexia?

Dyslexia is reading, writing, spelling or saying letters or words in reverse. Dyslexia in spelling means poor spelling plus writing letters in reverse. Poor spelling in English is caused by the illogical way English words are spelled. Only analyzers can become poor spellers in English and then acquire dyslexia in spelling; memorizers do not acquire dyslexia in reading or spelling. Being logical learners is hereditary but not being dyslexic. People are not born seeing or writing letters in reverse.

What is dyslexia in spelling and what causes it?

Dyslexia in spelling means poor spelling plus writing letters in reverse. While all types of dyslexia are caused by forced speed at some point and time, dyslexia in spelling and in writing letters in reverse is caused by forced speed-reading before learning to spell words. Dyslexia in spelling letters in reverse is an advanced stage of poor spelling. Poor spellers misspell words but dyslexic persons misspell words plus write letters in reverse.

Before the 4th grade, pupils whose learning style is a logical learning style become poor spellers; to them English spelling is illogical. Having spelling difficulties causes them to fall behind in class. By the 4th grade, they feel forced to speed-read to finish their schoolwork. Forced speed-reading leaves them no time to see the details inside the words they are reading. Their vision travels too fast from left to right and vice versa. In their haste, they see letters in reverse and then spell letters in reverse, in that same manner that they saw them and read them. They are forced to run before they can crawl or walk. Spelling difficulties persist into adolescence and adulthood with trouble memorizing without logic and with reading aloud. The equation looks like this: Spelling Difficulties + Forced Speed-reading → Dyslexia

The Six Steps that Cause Dyslexia in English Spelling

Dyslexia in spelling and in writing letters in reverse is given to kids before the 4th grade, but only logical learners can have it, and what causes it is lack of logical spelling rules and being compelled to speed-read before learning to spell words. Reading too fast, too soon causes persons with spelling difficulties to see letters in reverse, and eventually writing them in reverse.

Step 1: Logical Learners becoming Poor Spellers: Logical learners (analyzers) like, Albert Einstein who could not spell, are born with a brain that is wired to require logical explanations before they can memorize anything. Their learning style is a logical learning style and to them, the spelling of English words is illogical. Because they are logical; they may expect to see "My cat is cute." to be "Mi kat iz qut." If no logical explanations are provided, they cannot memorize the spelling of English words and they become poor spellers. Some analyzers cannot read at all.

Logical children who only know the ABC's are usually shocked when a great number of sentences like "My cat is cute." are randomly thrown at them to read in a story without any logical structure (whole language), and they wonder WHY they were told one thing when they were learning their ABC's and then expected to read or write another. It is because of this big WHY that logical learners / analyzers fall behind in class while memorizers are reading and spelling at a faster pace.

Step 2: Too Young to Form Complex Linguistic Questions: Because they are so young, children with a logical learning style cannot form all the complex linguistic questions they wish to ask about the illogical way words are spelled. They may wish to ask their teacher why the "i" sound is spelled with a "y" in "my," why the "k" sound is spelled with a "c" in "cat," why the "z" sound is spelled with an "s" in "is," and why the "q" sound is spelled with a "cu" in "cute"; but they cannot form such complex linguistic questions.

Eventually, they become too overwhelmed with the number of questions they wish to ask, and then they decide to keep their mouths shut and put the blame upon themselves.

Step 3: Falling Behind in Class: As a result, logical children continue to fall behind in class, and no one realizes why they are falling behind. No one else around them knows what they have been through; even they, themselves, lose track of what is taking place. This entire episode happens so fast; it is like a quick nightmare that one forgets its details after waking up.

Shortly after that, the commotion created around them and the worried parents lead these poor kids to believe they have some type of an innate learning problem. Before they know it, the testing specialists come to schools to diagnose them as dyslexics and / or learning disabled. Their only fault is that they are too intelligent to accept the illogical way English words are spelled.

Their condition remains a mystery to them, to their teachers, to their parents, and even to the specialists who may have a PhD in dyslexia diagnostic. According to reliable statistics, 2 out of 3 people have dyslexia in English. It is an outrage to watch our nation's finest type of thinkers being forced to live with dyslexia and falling behind in class. Since when was questioning, analyzing, and logical thinking a defect? In time, these unfortunate kids fall behind, not only in reading and spelling but also in all other subjects that require reading and spelling. This explains why so many dyslexic persons are creative in performing arts that do not require as much reading or spelling. Type "Celebrities with Dyslexia" in search engines and you will need hours to read the long list.

Step 4: Feeling the Need to hurry to catch up with Schoolwork: Consequently, analyzers become aware of the need to hurry, and they read faster to keep up with their classmates who are memorizers. They feel the pressure of having to read faster coming from their school, their peers, their parents, and from society at large. They are told to try harder, and traditional educators and other literacy advocates advise these kids to speed-read, and to read more interesting stories to improve their spelling skills.

Traditional educators have no idea that kids with a logical learning style cannot focus on two things at a time; namely, they cannot focus simultaneously on the way words are spelled, while reading for comprehension.

Step 5: Forced Speed-reading before Learning to Spell Words Causes Dyslexia: Traditional educators continue to ask logical kids to read more stories when these poor kids cannot yet read or spell words or certain sounds in words. Nevertheless, kids continue to try harder to read as they are told. In the midst of all this pressure, they develop the ability to speed-read before learning to spell or read words.

Eventually, these kids speed-read without seeing the way words are spelled and they do not have time to see the details inside words and differentiate words like (niece & nice), (nose & noise), (exit & exist) or (united & untied). They are highly focused on the main idea and don't have the time needed to look and see the details inside the words they are reading. They hurry so much that their vision travels rapidly from left-to-right and from right-to-left. **In their haste, they end up seeing letters and sometimes words in reverse. When they write, they hurry and reverse letters, in that same reversed manner that they saw them and read them.**

These logical kids are in a desperate need to read slowly in order to see the way words are written. Yet, they feel forced to speed-read, and speed-reading only worsens their situation. Speed in reading or in anything is a result of a process that one can only achieve naturally; speed cannot be achieved through force. We cannot force babies to run before they can crawl or walk.

Step 6: Can Only Focus on One Thing at a Time: Constantly, dyslexic persons think they have to hurry, and they become obsessed with hurrying. If dyslexia is a disorder, it is an acquired hurrying disorder that can be reversed. Even when asked to look at words and copy them, they hurry and may copy letters in reverse. They hurry more when asked to find the main idea in the story or when asked to pay attention to punctuation or grammar. Logical learners (analyzers) can only focus on one thing at a time; hence, they focus highly on the main idea but not on the way, words are spelled. And this is the story of how dyslexia is given to kids before the 4th grade.

Read Teachers' Responses: When groups of teachers were initially asked if there was anything wrong with asking **all** kids to read "My cat is cute."; all agreed that there was no problem with this sentence, and that they would continue to ask young children to read more such simple sentences in children's books. It is true that those who are visual learners born with a brain wired to memorize anything without questioning the logic behind it would learn to read and spell "My cat is cute." However, when the same groups of teachers became aware that there were logical learners, they changed their minds. Some expressed that they were aware of different learning styles but not of logical learners. Most were trained to think that the two different learning styles meant kids with or without learning disabilities. Others expressed they were aware of visual or oral learners but had not heard of logical learners. A few of the teachers who struggled with spelling themselves admitted that they had dyslexia and that this was exactly what happened to them when they were growing up; one said this presentation was like telling my life story.

The 15 Major Characteristics Shared by Dyslexic Persons

These characteristics reveal that dyslexic persons can learn and are not learning disabled; they are logical learners that learn logically. They can only focus on one thing or one thought at a time. They are not visual and cannot visualize faces or the way words are spelled. They are perfectionists needing a long time to finish their work; all work to them must be creative or they may not finish it. They tend to become unhappy when disturbed while doing their creative work. Most dyslexic persons misspell words, write letters in reverse, stumble when reading aloud, have difficulties spelling words orally, miss their exists if driving and someone is talking with them, have accidents when text messaging and driving, and some write all of the letters in uppercase.

1. Writing Letters in Reverse: Dyslexia in spelling is paired with spelling difficulties and with writing letters in reverse.

2. Stumble when Reading Aloud: Dyslexia in reading is paired with reading difficulties. Some cannot read at all; others may read and comprehend but stumble when reading aloud.

3. Being Logical Learners: Dyslexic persons are born analytic, too logical to accept nonsense. Logical learners question the way English words are spelled, and they may never accept the illogical way words are spelled. Their learning style is a logical learning style. If logic is provided they can easily learn to read and spell.

4. Can Focus Only on One Thing at a Time: Dyslexic persons can only focus on one thing or one thought at a time; for instance, they cannot focus both on the main idea in a story and on the way, words are spelled. Most dyslexic persons are unaware of this fact until it is brought to their attention. They focus so highly on one thing, that they often become very creative at that one thing.

5. They Need Not be Disturbed: Typically, when dyslexic persons are busy doing something that requires focus, they need not be disturbed. If disturbed, they may become unhappy or angry.

6. Autistic Persons are Similar But: Autistic persons may have a fit when disturbed. Autistic persons are similar in this respect, but they are much more focused on one thing at a time. Their reaction can be much more dramatic. Autistic persons can be so highly focused on one thing that when someone calls their name, they may not respond.

7. Perfectionists, take a Very Long Time to finish their Creative Work: Dyslexic persons tend to be perfectionists in the subject they choose to focus on and they take a very long time to finish their creative work. To them, everything they focus on has to be perfect or they let it go. When a dyslexic child is busy being creative, she or he feels like saying, "Leave me alone, I am being creative here, and you are disturbing my train of thoughts."

8. Dyslexic Drivers tend to Miss Their Exits When Disturbed: More often than not, when driving and someone is talking with them or distracting them, dyslexic drivers tend to miss their exits because they cannot focus on both, the conversation and the driving directions.

9. Born to Think a Single Thought! No Text Messaging! In addition to being born unable to do two things at a time, dyslexic persons cannot think two thoughts at a time. Because they cannot think about two things simultaneously, when text messaging or talking on the phone while driving, even if hands are free, dyslexic drivers will most likely have accidents. They are simply born with the ability to think a single thought at a time, not two.

10. Extremely Creative at that one Thing of Their Focus: Normally, when dyslexic persons are allowed the time needed to focus on that one thing that they like to focus on, they become extremely creative at that one thing of their focus.

Dyslexic persons are logical learners, too intelligent to accept the illogical way English words are spelled. This explains seeing high creativity among dyslexic persons; but, not so much among good spellers, who can memorize without questioning the logic in the thing they are about to memorize. Such good spellers' attention is disbursed on multiple tasks, unable to focus on only one task to the point of becoming highly creative at it.

Albert Einstein could not spell and he is a fine example of such highly focused and creative persons. Additional examples of such creative and analytic persons who have dyslexia are Thomas Edison, William Faulkner, James Joyce, Agatha Christie, Nelson Rockefeller, Thomas Jefferson, Walt Dizny, Bill Gates, Henry Winkler, Robin Williams, Tom Cruise, Steve Jobs, Whoopi Goldberg, Jay Leno, Anderson Cooper, Ben Affleck, and the list is too long to list here. Type "famous people with dyslexia" in search engines and you will need hours, if not days, to read the long lists.

11. Not Visuals and cannot focus on Details inside Words: Dyslexic persons are not visuals and cannot visualize faces or images; this means they cannot visualize the way a word is spelled. Therefore, they may have difficulties spelling a long word orally. Instead, they may write it down to spell it. In addition, when they speed-read before learning to spell words, they do not have the time needed to see additional details, such as punctuation and grammar.

12. Writing All Letters in Uppercase: If a person writes all letters in uppercase, then most likely she or he is dyslexic or has the potential to become dyslexic. However, not all dyslexic persons write their letters in uppercase.

13. Shared Characteristics and General Behavior: Dyslexia manifests itself in the person's general behavior and characteristics. Understanding dyslexia makes it is easy to tell if a person is dyslexic or if a child might become dyslexic.

14. Being a Logical Learner is Hereditary but not being Dyslexic: Dyslexic persons are logical learners and being a logical learner is hereditary but not being dyslexic. If they were born into a language that has a single letter to spell a sound every time that sound is written, logical learners would not have dyslexia in that language.

15. Dyslexia and Learning Disabilities: Dyslexic persons do NOT have learning disabilities nor do they have neurological learning deficiencies; perhaps those who don't understand them do. There are now proofs for that. Lee's dyslexia was easily and quickly reversed; see how <u>Lee Learned to Read in a Week!</u> Not only did Lee learn and prove he was NOT learning disabled; but also he learned in six days what his school could not teach him in six years.

How much is known about dyslexia?

In spite of the enormous amount of money being spent on dyslexia, researchers and traditional educators know very little about it. When I approached someone who had a PhD in dyslexia, he said there was no known solution for dyslexia and thus his specialty was not in finding answers, but in conducting tests in schools to diagnose children who had dyslexia. If a child cannot read or spell, parents are usually informed that their child has dyslexia and left at that. Most parents wonder whether this is a biological or an environmental problem. When they turn to traditional educators, they are not told their child is an analyzer whose learning style is a logical learning style; instead, parents are left with more confusion than they initially had.

Al Graham, age 44 was Sadik's student at Cuyamaca College in 1999. Al said, "Both of my parents were professors at SDSU and they tried hundreds of tutors and teachers and everyone gave up on me. They said I had dyslexia, learning disabilities, possible brain injury due to a motorcycle accident, and a bunch of things." Years after the class had ended, Al wrote, "I took the CBEST and past it the first time, all three sections. I know you know this but you probably still enjoy hearing it, that your class I think got me and is getting me through my spelling difficulties. I will always be thankful! I really feel your program is helping make the difference in my success." Al is currently a first-grade teacher teaching phonics and spelling in the same way that he learned.

Common Misconceptions about Dyslexia

1. Some argue that dyslexia is hereditary and thus it cannot be acquired. Reality is that being analytic is indeed hereditary, but not being dyslexic. In fact, when phonics is taught logically and comprehensively with over 100 spelling rules, analytics do not become poor spellers and do not acquire dyslexia in spelling.

2. Others claim that dyslexic persons have trouble hearing the sounds correctly and thus misspell words. I am certain they can hear the long ē sound but do not know which of the 10 spelling patterns to choose when spelling it in words, as in meet, meat, media, receipt, chief, complete, ski, machine, happy, and attorney. I am certain they can hear the "f" sound but do not know which of the three spelling patterns to choose when spelling it, as in font, symphony, and tough.

3. There are parents that still think their dyslexic kids are too lazy to learn. Reality is that it is not a matter of choice for these kids and no they are not lazy–their logical minds cannot memorize without regularity. Their brains reject such inconsistent spelling patterns of the same sound in so many different words.

4. The vast majority of traditional educators have not heard of people having a logical learning style; they are trained to accept poor reading and spelling skills in English as a learning disability. Some do know that when logic is provided, analyzers learn to spell, but they had not heard that English has except five spelling rules like the trivial "i before e except after c rule."

5. Some researchers see two different biological and functional structures in the brains of dyslexic persons and good spellers. Also, they see dyslexic persons having trouble learning to read or spell, and they wrongly conclude that dyslexic persons have neurological learning deficiencies. They need yet to realize that seeing different patterns in the brain does not entail deficiency and that being different is not the same as being defected. They need yet to realize that dyslexic persons do learn to read and spell when logic is provided.

Raising Students' Self-esteem because They are the Better Thinkers

From the first day of class, teachers need to inform students who have difficulties reading or spelling that the problem is not in them, but it is precisely in the fact that one English sound is spelled in so many different ways. Most students were wrongly led to believe they had learning disabilities or neurological learning deficiencies. Immediately, they need to stop blaming themselves for not remembering the correct spelling of words or certain sounds in words. Let these little geniuses know that poor spellers are the better thinkers because they are analyzers and that they simply require logical answers to everything that does not make sense.

Offering Concrete Solutions to the Spelling Problems

Offer your students actual solutions that will help them learn and learn quickly. Show them examples of spelling rules and of phonics lessons to prove to them that they can now learn to spell hundreds of words at a time.

Study the 100 spelling rules and the 600 phonics lessons in the books to be ready to answer all of their logical questions about spelling a word one-way and not the other. Assure them they will remember how to spell naturally and without forced memorization.

Why parent must get involved?

Parents must get involved because teaching phonics is a process that requires much more time than simply teaching the ABC's. No teacher has the time needed to teach a child to read and spell 180 spelling patterns of 90 sounds in 32,000 words. Obviously, our schools have not been able to do it alone; otherwise, we wouldn't have had such high illiteracy rate. Teachers may recommend these phonics-based reading and spelling books to parents, and most parents will be more than happy to get involved.

Teach Vowels First to Babies and Toddlers

If you are a parent of babies or toddlers, you need not start with teaching the ABC's; instead, begin with the five long vowels a, e, i, o, and u. Presenting 26 letters together will only confuse them and slow them down. Teach vowels first to help them speak sooner and eventually read sooner. All words contain, at least, one vowel sound and when they learn to say the five vowels, you can stick any other letter to the vowels to help them say a countless number of small words. For instance, if they know how to say "o" you can easily help them to say "toe."

The Creative Ones

More than half of the population cannot focus on the way words are spelled while reading for comprehension. In fact, analyzers cannot focus on any two things or two thoughts at a time. Traditional teachers are unaware of this fact; thus, they continue to ask students who cannot spell to read more interesting stories, hoping that in the process students will learn to spell.

The main reason most poor spellers are more creative is that they can focus highly on one thing at a time and then can become creative in that one thing of their focus. Albert Einstein could not spell and he is a fine example of such highly focused and creative persons.

Teachers or parents need to inform students who have difficulties reading or spelling that unlike them, memorizers cannot focus on one thing like they do; thus, they are less capable and less likely to become creative in any one subject–usually, their attention is too scattered to enable them to be creative in one subject.

There are certain characteristic and signals to identify analyzers in your classrooms–one of them is that they are the creative ones. Parents may raise their kid's self-esteem by changing the naming of "dyslexic" to "analyzer" or the "creative one."

The way teachers or parents deal with dyslexic persons has a huge impact them. When students are let down too many times, they may give up on learning all together, and there is enough evidence suggesting that traditional teaching is what veers dyslexic persons away from learning.

Poor Spellers know a Good Spelling Curriculum when They See It

Students ought to be involved in choosing the appropriate spelling curriculum in their school or home. According to reliable statistics, half of the adults in the U.S. are unable to read books written at an eighth-grade level. This makes the literates elites less than half of the population. Because they are memorizers and can spell, the literate elites often end up becoming the decision makers, deciding the teaching methodologies and the reading and spelling curriculum taught in schools. Naturally, they choose whole language over phonics because of the way they had learned to read and spell when they were growing up. They cannot always be sensitive enough to the needs of students with a logical learning style because they do not know what that means. Such teachers were trained by traditional teaching styles that were also designed by memorizers.

Notoriously, such teachers argue that teaching whole language is better because reading comprehension is what counts most. Not all of them were informed that teaching phonics is only a step that does not last but a few weeks or months. Using *Read Instantly* by Camilia Sadik, students learn to read within hours or days and using *Learn to Spell 500 Words a Day*, students learn to spell 13,000 words within days or weeks. Moreover, whenever teachers teach a lesson or two from these books, students take minutes to decide this is the curriculum for them.

Because literacy is a very serious issue, the literate elites who have not "felt" or "known" how others learn, need not be the ones choosing the spelling curriculum. People with spelling difficulties, even if they are young kids, need to be seriously involved in choosing their own curriculum. They may be asked to review and compare all the available spelling programs, and they will easily recognize the appropriate ones.

> Poor spellers know best and they need to be seriously involved in choosing their own spelling curriculum.

Analyzers are constantly looking for programs that offer answers to their logical way of thinking, and they know best what works and what does not work for them. Their ultimate dream is to find some regularity in English.

Living an Entire Life with Dyslexia

Some dyslexic persons may "get by" with reading but have difficulties spelling the words that they read. Others may not learn to read at all. If they did not learn to read or spell by the end of the 3rd grade, chances are they are not going to learn from traditional learning methods. According to them, memorizing without logic is impossible. Their minds will never open up to the illogical way words are written and they will continue their search for programs that offer them logical spelling rules. With logical explanations, dyslexic persons read aloud a 152-page book entitled *Read Instantly* by Camilia Sadik in less within hours or days.

Except in arts, music, and some divisions of science, dyslexic persons will naturally suffer from low performances and low grades in the subjects that require reading and writing in English. They often express their sorrow from the way society looks down at them or blames them. The saddest part is that too many dyslexic persons tend to think society is right and that they are to blame because they did not do it right when they were little kids.

Society owes them a huge apology. Millions suffer from low self-esteem and books can be written about dyslexic persons' heartbreaking life stories. Before the labeling of "learning disability" was accepted in schools, children were told they were too lazy to study. Isn't time to try to make up for some of the damage done in the past? Should we keep the name "dyslexia" that rhymes with medical conditions like anorexia, asphyxia, hysteria, etc.? I suggest changing the naming of "dyslexia" to "analytic strictness," and changing "dyslexics" to "analytics."

Solutions to Prevent or End Dyslexia in Spelling and in Reversing Letters

1. Understanding Dyslexia is half of the Solution: Understanding dyslexia and how dyslexia is given to people is half of the solution to reversing or ending dyslexia is in spelling. Understanding dyslexia also means diagnosing it and choosing the best available curriculum for it. For testimonials from young and old students, teachers of K-12, and adult literacy teachers, please visit SpellingRules.com. You may teach or learn the spelling of **820** words instantly while visiting SpellingRules.com!

Lee Learned to Read in a Week! Lee, a sixth grader, had dyslexia and could not read or spell words. Not only did Lee learn but also he learned in a week. Because he learned so quickly, Lee proved he was NOT learning disabled. His school never did understand how he learned when prior to that he was sitting in class for six years unable to read. After Lee learned to read and spell, his teacher Mr. Woods expressed, "Lee seems to be calculating something before he can spell words, and I don't care how he gets them as long as he keeps spelling them right."

2. Dyslexia can be Ended: It is much easier to prevent dyslexia in K-3, because the older people become the more logical they become. Besides, it is always easier to do than to undo. Nevertheless, dyslexia can be ended through learning phonics logically, utilizing the logic in the 100 spelling rules that are applied in 600 phonics lessons, and reading all the practice lessons aloud slowly. Moreover, slowing down is a necessary step to stop the progress of seeing and then writing letters in reverse. Dyslexic persons were forced to run before they could crawl and walk; they will not recover from that unless they return to the crawling stage. To end or reverse other types of dyslexia, go back to the crawling stage. For instance, dyslexia in speech was caused by intimidations and forced speed; and, the solution to that is going back to the crawling stage. Try to throw out the causes that used to intimidate you and start a new–train yourself to speak slowly.

3. Dyslexia can be Prevented: Dyslexia can be easily prevented by parents before sending kids to school. The principle of *Informing before Introducing* is applied throughout *Read Instantly* by Camilia Sadik. Teach phonics right after teaching the ABC's and right before asking K-3 kids to read sentences and stories. In *Read Instantly*, over 180 spelling patterns of phonics are placed in a queue and then introduced logically, one-at-a-time, and in a group of 20 to 50 words. Each lesson is carefully planned and no lesson is placed there arbitrarily. Using this little book entitled *Read Instantly* is the key to preventing dyslexia before the 4th grade. When the principle of *Informing before Introducing* is practiced in schools and in homes, our children would have no reason to acquire dyslexia.

It is important to teach all of the spelling patterns of phonics, not only bits and pieces of them. For instance, don't ask student to read "cian" as in "musician" until "cian" reaches its turn in the queue and students are informed that "cian" is used in words that refer to careers or hobbies. Since "cian" occurs in 17 English words, show them a comprehensive list of these words, as in electrician, pediatrician, mathematician, etc.

Teach phonics as if you were teaching the rest of the ABC's. Only after phonics is taught, should we ask analytic learners to read and write sentences, stories, or any other form of a written text. If an adult is learning to read, follow the same steps. Remember that adults need to go back to the crawling step that they missed when they were growing up.

Teaching phonics is only a step that does not take but weeks or months, depending on the level you are teaching. When dyslexia is understood, it will be easily prevented within hours or days of a tutor's time.

Cases of ADD caused by Dyslexia can Easily End

Reading is the foundation for all learning. Obviously a dyslexic child forced to sit in classrooms year-after-year, without learning and participating in class activities, is going to be bored to the point of developing ADD.

B.J. could read but could not spell; and he recovered from ADD after studying in my spelling class for 10 days. Months later, I ran into him and his father. He said, "My grades are all straight A's now Ms. Sadik." B.J.'s overflowing energy was reversed into positive energy. Anticipate seeing a separate book written by Camilia Sadik about the life stories of those who used to have dyslexia or ADD or ADHD.

Parents please do not accept medicating your children who have ADD! Give them this logical learning opportunity first. It is an outrage to drug perfectly normal kids and to cause them to live with awful side effects.

Sample Lesson for Preventing Dyslexia taken from *Read Instantly* by Camilia Sadik

- ✔ Teachers: **I**nform **b**efore **I**ntroducing these spelling pattern of phonics made by the letter "**y**":
  - The "y" at the beginning of words or syllables, sounds like a consonant: yes, yard
  - The "y" at the end of short words, sounds like the long vowel ī: by, my, fly, why
  - The "y" at the end of long words, sounds like the long vowel ē: hap·py, his·to·ry
  - The "ey" at the end of words, sounds like the long vowel ē: key, mon·key, val·ley
  - The "ay" sounds like the long vowel ā: play, day, stay
  - The special sound of "ōy": boy, toy, joy, en·joy
  - The "y" sounds like the long vowel ī at the end of stressed syllables: by·pass
  - The "y" sounds like the long vowel ī as in: style
  - The "y" in the middle of syllables can sound like short ĭ: Lynn, gym, gymnasium

- ✔ Students: Read aloud slowly to memorize these words that contain the "y" as a vowel:

my	why	by	sly	shy
fun·ny	hap·py	hap·pi·ly	car·ry	hur·ry
key	mon·key	don·key	val·ley	al·ley
day	play	way	tray	say
boy	toy	em·ploy	joy	en·joy

A Few Testimonials and More are Available on SpellingRules.com

Lee Ray Nachman, age 12, grade 6, first-grade reading level (level 1.6), Lassen View Union Elementary School, Red Bluff, California. Lee was repeatedly told he had dyslexia, ADD, and learning disabilities. In just six days, Lee learned to read. Eight months after that, Lee learned to spell. His ADD vanished. Not only did Lee learn but also he learned in a week. Because he learned so quickly, Lee proved that he was NOT learning disabled and that he did not need medications for his ADD. You may see Lee's handwriting before and after and watch his video on SpellingRules.com

Eleazar Herrera, age 11, grade 6 from Cajon Valley School District, El Cajon, CA where Sadik taught a two-week pilot program. Eleazar's pre-spelling test was 19/100 and after 12 hours of classroom instructions, he scored 90/100. Eleazar said, "I was used to reading without looking at the way words are spelled because my other teachers always told me to read fast. I thought I could never learn to spell. Spelling isn't as difficult as I thought it was. I wish someone had told me about these spelling rules before."

Natalie Munno, age 15, grade 9 from The Charter School of San Diego. Her pre-test was 41/100 and after a total of 11 hours of classroom instructions, she scored 100/100. Natalie said, "In the future, I will teach my kids to spell." Natalie went on to say, "I didn't learn how to read until I was in the fourth grade and I never learned how to spell. This class helped me learn to spell. I especially liked Ms. Sadik's techniques for remembering things." Natalie said she would absolutely participate in this class again. "I'd do it in a heartbeat."

B.J. Penick, age 13, grade 8 from The Charter School of San Diego. His pre-test 50/100 and after nine hour of classroom instructions, he scored 99/100 on a post-test. B. J. said, "Now, I know how to spell. Spelling is easy. Ask me any words, and I will spell them." B.J.'s father said, "My son is learning the spelling of thousands of words everyday and his vocabulary is increasing." A year later, B.J. and his father expressed that he was one of the best students in his class. He said, "I get straight A's in every class."

Brian, age 9, grade 4, from Irvine, CA, 2011. Brian's Mother who is a schoolteacher said, "Brian cannot not use his hands to write words and his school had accepted him living with a keyboard for the rest of his life. In less than two hours, Sadik taught Brian to spell 20 words logically, gave him a mechanical pencil with a big eraser to erase whenever he wanted, and then asked him to write only one of the 20 words he learned. Brian handwrote all 20 words and he turned out to have the most beautiful handwriting. Obviously, Brian used to scribble to avoid misspelling and to protest the inconsistency in the way we spell phonics in words. When asked how did you do it? Brian replied, 'It's this pencil.'"

Rosie - Amazon verified purchase of Learn to Spell 500 Words a Day: The Vowel A. Rosie wrote, "Excellent approach to learn to spell. "We are enjoying this book. I would highly recommend it if you are looking at a good approach for spelling and learning some of the rules as well. In my opinion, this is a great series of books for parents to use at home with their children. The way that it is organized makes teaching and learning spell easy."

Lisa Miller, wife of Dyslexic Husband - Amazon verified purchase of Read Instantly. Lisa wrote, "What a blessing! Purchased this book after searching tirelessly for an answer to my dilemma. This book has helped my dyslexic husband to be confident in his desire to finally help himself read! I believe that Camilia Sadik is a true hero; she has developed a way of teaching that makes sense to otherwise hopeless feeling students. Would highly recommend this book to anyone of any age struggling with reading. It's our little miracle book! Thank you Ms. Sadik!"

Testimonials from Inmates and Other Attendees: After teaching a three-hour spelling course to inmates with spelling difficulties and dyslexia in Kansas City, Missouri, attendees had this to say:

Leslie Riggs, State Attorney for the prison system and for Charter Schools wrote, Leslie wrote, "Camilia: I am pleased that you have found a life's work that promises to help so many people. I am glad you came to America."

Nancy Leaser, Prison Superintendent, Nancy said, "My wish is for Camilia to come back to Missouri, to teach our inmates, train our teachers, and put me out of business."

Inmates Students expressed the following before the books were published:
• Can we keep this book?

• Can we buy this book in a bookstore?

• Will you promise to come back?

• If you aren't coming back, will you remember to tell us where we can get this book?

• Here are our names and addresses to let us know where we can get this book after you publish it. Please promise not to forget us.

• Remember me! Remember me!

• I love this; I can use these big words when I write letters."

They expressed the feeling that big words had only been accessible to a certain class of people, but not to them. Now, the opportunity was open to them!

Carol Stevens Spelling Demystified**, a Satisfied Tutor of a brain-injured person, Amazon verified purchase of Read Instantly, "I purchased this book to use with a brain injured client because he has to learn to spell and read all over again. He was confused by the many exceptions to the seemingly innumerable spelling rules/exceptions in our English language. Although the title says Read Instantly, the explanations of the sounds in English mesh naturally with many spelling rules. The order of letters, words and phonic sounds taught builds slowly but steadily to give mastery at every level. Some of the instructions to the teacher are repetitive and not all that helpful, but an experienced teacher will not be hindered by this. In fact, my client began reading the teacher's directions on his own and practically taught himself the content. Try this with anyone who has even the slightest difficulty with reading and spelling. Home school moms and dads, this would work great with children from beginner to intermediate readers who are having difficulty."

Testimonials from Adult Literacy Teachers at the COABE Convention in 1999: After giving a workshop during the 1999 National Convention of Commission on Adult Basic Education (COABE), Adult literacy teachers wrote their evaluations of Camilia Sadik's workshop:

• Thank you, Camilia for teaching me how to better teach my students

• Bring her back next year!!! Exciting approach, informative

• Thank you. Keep on telling people that English spelling makes sense.

• She needs a bigger room. Excellent!

• I can't wait to order the book! Thank you so much. Great information!

• Elaine said, "I wish to open Camilia's head to see inside and learn how it works."

• This presentation was superb and has certainly great information that will be helpful for my students and for myself.

• **Nancy Merrill, Kansas City School District** wrote, "I am on the Language Arts Curriculum Work Team for the Kansas City, Missouri School District. I don't know yet if you truly realize the scope of what you have done. Your program is sensible, yet comprehensive. Bravo!!!!"

More Testimonials: There are more testimonials, too many to list here. An entire book can be written about our testimonials and the life stories of those affected by spelling difficulties that we have helped.

No known person has escaped learning from Linguist Camilia Sadik's books. The 30 unique learning features in her books have made learning to read and spell logical and possible for all types of learners, whether they do or do not have dyslexia.

Dyslexic persons do NOT have learning disabilities or neurological learning deficiencies; perhaps those who don't understand them do!

Finally, yet importantly, too many people are falsely led to believe that dyslexic persons are born with learning disabilities; but now that we know that dyslexia is not hereditary and how dyslexia in reading and spelling English words is given to kids before the 4th grade, we know that dyslexic persons are not born with learning disabilities.

If dyslexic persons had learning disabilities, how do we explain Lee learning to read in a week? Because Lee learned to read a week, Lee proved that dyslexic persons do NOT have neurological learning deficiencies, and that they do NOT have learning disabilities, but perhaps those who don't understand them do.

Perhaps analyzers like Lee can help memorizers learn to analyze and question things that they believe in. As it turns out, Lee's ADD was a result of boredom from sitting in class for six years, unable to read or participate in learning. Again, parents beware of medicating your kids who have ADD, because ADD that is caused by spelling difficulties or dyslexia will naturally end after learning to read and spell logically.

Conclusion

Dyslexia in spelling or reading is acquired but only by analytic learners, and what causes it is being compelled to speed-read before learning to spell words. Reading too fast, too soon causes poor spellers to see letters in reverse and eventually writing letters in reverse.

Lack of Logic → Spelling Difficulties among Logical Learners: The inconsistency in the way we spell phonics in words causes spelling difficulties among logical learners. The learning style of logical learners is that they need logic to decide whether to spell a same sound, one-way and not the other. Without logic, they cannot memorize whether to spell a "w" sound as in "choir" with a "w" or an "o." Lack of logic causes logical learners to have spelling difficulties, and eventually they end up falling behind in class.

Spelling Difficulties + Forced Speed-reading → Dyslexia in Reversing Letters: After they fall behind in class, kids who cannot spell feel pressured to read in a hurry to catch up with their schoolwork. They are forced to speed-read before learning to read or spell words. In their haste, they see letters in reverse and then spell letters in reverse, in that same manner that they saw them and read them.

Dyslexia in Spelling before the 4rd Grade: Kids with reading and /or spelling difficulties are usually diagnosed with dyslexia in the 4th grade. Logical learners are the ones who become poor spellers and then acquire dyslexia in spelling before the 4rd grade.

The 10 Phonics-based Spelling Books for all Ages by Linguist Camilia Sadik

Book 1: *Read Instantly* - 200 Logical Phonics Lessons for all Ages

This book is to teach phonics, and in it lies the groundwork for learning the rules that govern phonics. Anyone capable of learning the ABC's is guaranteed to learn to read from this book. Each vowel is dissected and isolated in a chapter in the second half of this book. Parents can now teach reading before sending kids to schools. This book is for beginners, but all learners need to start with it to learn phonics in a brand-new way.

Book 2: *Learn to Spell 500 Words a Day* (6 volumes: A, E, I, O, U, and Consonants)

Vowels are inconsistent, they rule English, and they cannot be avoided. In this book, each vowel is dissected and isolated in a volume. The eight consonants c, g, h, q, s, x, w, and y are also inconsistent; and they are isolated in a volume. Each lesson begins with a spelling rule, followed by a list of the words that follow that rule, followed by comprehensive and detailed practice lessons, and students are asked to read aloud to memorize the spelling of hundreds of words at a time. This book is for the intermediate level, ideal for grades 4-12 and for adult learners.

Book 3: *100 Spelling Rules*

Each spelling rule in this book is followed by a list of nearly all the words that follow it. Advanced students learn to spell hundreds of words from this book. Sadik's books are cumulative, and the book *100 Spelling Rules* is a book for the advance level.

Book 4: *The Compound Words* - 7,000 Compound and Hyphenated Words

Unlike looking up words in a dictionary, over 5,000 compound words and 2,000 hyphenated words are isolated in this book, grouped alphabetically, colored, and prepared for adults and children to read and learn. As in "rustproof," a compound word is composed of two or more words. As in "face-to-face," a hyphenated word is made of the two or more words, separated by hyphens.

Book 5: *How to Teach Phonics - Teachers' Guide*

This guide is for teachers, parents, or adult learners. It contains explanations of the teaching methodology and the symbols and concepts used in the books. In it are dyslexia solutions, spelling tests, and more. *Read more* SpellingRules.com

How to purchase books by Camilia Sadik

SpellingRules.com   Amazon.com   Bookstores Worldwide

About the Author

Linguist Camilia Sadik spent 15 years intensely dissecting English, discovering over 100 spelling rules, applying the rules in 600 phonics-based spelling lessons, class-testing her discoveries and preparing learning books for children and adults to read and spell hundreds of words at a time. The 30 unique learning features in Sadik's book make learning to read and spell inescapable. Sadik worked hard to make spelling easy and possible for all ages and all types of learners. In addition, Sadik found an easy solution to end dyslexia in spelling and in writing letters in reverse. Learning to spell and slowing down to write words slowly ends dyslexia.

Sadik saw the details of English sounds and their various spelling patterns and used that in easy-to-use vowels and consonants books. See these examples:

The vowel **A** has 5 sounds that are spelled in 12 ways.

The vowel **E** has 7 sounds that are spelled in 17 ways.

The vowel **I** has 8 sounds that are spelled in 19 ways.

The vowel **O** has 12 sounds that are spelled in 20 ways.

The vowel **U** has 6 sounds that are spelled in 28 ways.

Eight **consonants** have 50 sounds that are spelled in 60 ways.

Academically, Sadik earned a BA in Philosophy from WSU and an MA in Applied Linguistics from SDSU. In addition, Sadik earned California Teaching Credentials and is certified in teaching ABE and ESL. Before writing books, Sadik spent over 10 years reading the best of the world's literature.

©1997 Camilia Sadik

CPSIA information can be obtained
at www.ICGtesting.com
Printed in the USA
FSHW020815151020
74718FS